Grace on the Arrow

Wisdom Keys for Women of Audacious Faith and the Men Who Love Them

DR. TY MCDONALD

WestBow Press books may be ordered through booksellers or by contacting:

WestBow Press
A Division of Thomas Nelson & Zondervan
1663 Liberty Drive
Bloomington, IN 47403
www.westbowpress.com
1 (866) 928-1240

ISBN: 978-1-9736-5688-3 (sc)
ISBN: 978-1-9736-5690-6 (hc)
ISBN: 978-1-9736-5689-0 (e)

Library of Congress Control Number: 2019903134

Print information available on the last page.

WestBow Press rev. date: 3/15/2019

This book is affectionately dedicated to my threefold cord of husband, mother, and children. My husband, Ronnie, is both my Lapidoth, the trimmer of my wick who keeps me burning brightly and great love of my life, and my Barak, my mighty warrior who fights for me and beside me. Thank you, Ronnie, for walking with me hand in hand.

My mother, Shirley, has been a constant support and encourager, loving me sacrificially and unconditionally. My three children—Micaela, Alexa, and Micah—are the rhythm, harmony, and melody of my life song. Thank you for your patience over the years while I worked to honor my call and serve my King while loving you.

To my four brothers, Keevan, Demar, Byron and Michael, thank you for your love and for all the material for the books I have yet to write—epic adventures make epic stories.

Also to my first church family, Brazos Valley Community Church of God, thank you for your constant love and unwavering support. To my BOLD Church, Bastrop, family, thank you for allowing me to serve you. Thanks to Pastor Don Davis and Dr. Valerie Bridgeman for training my hands to make war.

Special thanks to Victor Simon, who has been a spiritual father in ministry, and Joann Roberts, who has walked with me over the years as a mother in ministry. Thanks to Eric Von Copland, who as been a faithful mentor in the prophetic. Many thanks and multiplied blessings to my team of intercessors—thank you for watching on the walls and for warring for me. Also to Dr. Anthony and Anita Parrett for their constant encouragement and support.

Finally, thanks to my King and the one for whom my heart beats, Jesus Christ, who has held me and kept me until this time for all time. I praise His matchless name.

Contents

Prelude

Sprinkled throughout Biblical history, we find stories of ordinary women called by God to do extraordinary things. They were orators and poets; warriors and prophets; judges, pastors, and apostles; great women like Miriam, Esther, Huldah, Priscilla, and Junia. They were powerful women of reknown who pioneered great revivals and broke barriers for women.

This is a story inspired by those women and another remarkable woman, Deborah, who led Israel in a time of turmoil into victory over an oppressive enemy. This is her story, and this is my story. This is the story of women in leadership roles; of overcoming challenges by the grace of God; of learning to simply be. This is the story of the call to Kingdom work in man's world. It is the story of a woman's work. It is a story for women and girls, and for the men and boys who love them.

I hope that this story will inspire your story and the story of your daughters and of your daughter's daughters. We are arrows in the hand of the Creator God. We are the arrows, He is the archer. Grace flows from his hands to the arrow so that the arrow always hits the mark.

CHAPTER 1

When Women Rise

Then the sons of Israel again did evil in the sight of the LORD, after Ehud died. And the Lord sold them into the hand of Jabin king of Canaan, who reigned in Hazor; and the commander of His army was Sisera who lived in Harosheth-hagoyim. The sons of Israel cried to the LORD; for he had nine hundred iron chariots, and he oppressed the sons of Israel for severely for twenty years.

—JUDGES4:1–3

"You have a brain tumor."

The words paralyzed me as my husband and I sat in my doctor's office on Thanksgiving day. My doctor, a family friend, hugged me and cried as I sat emotionless. Time seemed to stand still as words of promise flooded my mind.

How can this be? I thought. *No one in my family has this. I've always had health challenges, but nothing life-threatening. What of all the unfulfilled words of promise the Lord has given me? I haven't yet done anything He said I would do!*

That's when it hit me. I couldn't die! I couldn't die because God could not lie.

With that revelation, in that moment, the diagnosis somehow made sense. All the delay somehow made sense. God hadn't told me this was coming, but He knew. God knew this diagnosis would come, and He'd prepared me to hear it, rebuke it, and overcome it by giving me words of promise ahead of time and out of time, so that I would have hope as I was going through it. All the days in the past when I felt rejected, all the days I felt overlooked, the days I longed to see the fulfillment of the promises, the days I felt I had disqualified myself in some way and prayed for things to change, God had seen me and had heard my prayers. Hearing and seeing where I was and where I was going, He simply said, "I love you. You are mine." When I cried out, "How long, Lord?" He replied quietly, "Trust me. I'm saying no for a reason."

The words of promise had tarried on purpose. Their purpose was not only to break chains, as I had thought, but to give hope to the chain-breaker as well as the character to sustain the gift. The promised platform was being formed in the fire. Even with this epiphany of the purpose and plan of God, however, I still had a battle to win in my mind.

After the diagnosis, I had to visit a neurosurgeon. My neurosurgeon was very matter-of-fact—quite different from our family doctor who had sat and cried with us as she delivered the news of the results of the first tests. Once again, my husband was with me, and he held my hand as the surgeon discussed the plan of action. There would be no chemotherapy or treatment for six months. The surgeon wanted to see if the tumor would grow and then afterward discuss how to proceed with treatment.

I hate waiting. To me, it seemed that I was always waiting on something. But I waited again, and I fought while I waited. For six months, the enemy would come and whisper to me that I would die, that I wouldn't see my children grow to adulthood, that I wouldn't finish the ministry work I began, that someone else would have my husband's faithful love. I had taught spiritual warfare to others, and I knew what to do. I knew that I needed to take the thoughts that were contrary to the word of God captive, but I couldn't. My brain was too full of cynical thoughts, and my head was too full of pain.

Fortunately, my husband was with me. We had been married since our early twenties, and he knew the words of promise that had been spoken over my life. When the battle in my mind became intense and I felt depression and the spirit of heaviness trying to overtake me, my husband would come and remind me of the promise.

"Have you traveled to nations?" he asked.

"No."

"Have you seen limbs restored and blind eyes opened? Has your shadow transferred the anointing?" he continued.

"No," I would answer, with a smile each time. I was drawing from his strength.

"Then you can't die. And that's that!" he proclaimed. I was thankful to God for placing this man in my life as my husband.

My mother was also a constant encourager, even though I could see deep concern in her face. She often laid hands on me to pray for me during those six months. My church family also fought for me when I couldn't fight for myself. They fasted and prayed while I was eating. They fought for me like warriors.

So many fought for me. Several pastors from neighboring churches in the city gathered to pray for me. It had always been my desire, and I had tried several times, to gather the area pastors together to pray for our city apart from the annual National Day of Prayer that seemed too political to me to be impactful. Even though I was allowed by our local Ministerial Alliance to lead the National Day of Prayer for our county for a few years, I sensed that there was more that we should do.

After leading a National Day of Prayer gathering one year, I walked into a Ministerial Alliance meeting late and discerned that I was the topic of discussion. This was confirmed when the speaker who had the floor continued to talk about how we should change the scope of the prayer so that the alliance received credit and not any one individual. I sensed that there were some who misjudged my motives and felt that I was leading the prayer—which drew more and more participants each year—to advance my own congregation.

That was a painful revelation, because I love my Father. I love talking to Him in prayer and teaching others to pray, and I loved my city and the churches there. I had a desire to see them all, and the Kingdom, advancing. Afterward, I still desired a gathering, but that gathering never happened. Part of me felt that because I was a woman, they would not gather when I called. I felt the bitter sting of nonacceptance.

But this time, in the greatest battle of my life, they came. And they came in numbers, in unity and in force. Even ones who were part of denominations that did not accept women in ministry came to pray. I was overwhelmed by this and felt the love of my Father encompass me as the pastors, my colleagues, and my husband circled around me and prayed.

After six months, I had another MRI. When I went in for the results, the neurosurgeon, who had been Spock-like in the previous appointment, had a joyful but perplexed look on his face.

"We have your results," he said. "We cannot find the tumor. I am releasing you. Just come back in six months for a checkup." I thanked him, grabbed my husband's hand, and ran out of the office. God had healed me. I felt His love. I felt encompassed by His love. I knew I'd never see that adversary again.

Leaders Are Not Born But Made

On the way to destiny, there will always be adversaries. An adversary rises to cause a crisis that forces the rise of a leader. Throughout human history, we see this leadership pattern where a need arises and people makes themselves available to meet the need. There is a problem, and someone rises to solve it. There is a giant, and someone rises to face him. The problem, challenge, or adversary is often the teacher that appears when the student is ready.

You are the student. You recognize the enemy. You see the problem. You're not afraid of the giant. But you say to yourself, who am I to step up? Surely there are many who are vastly more qualified than I. I'm a soccer mom. I'm a teacher. I'm an executive. I'm qualified for this and not for that.

You read the story of Miriam who, with her brothers, led millions of people out of a place of struggle into a place of opportunity, and you're inspired. You read of Deborah, the prophet and judge in Israel who led her people into victory over their enemy as a mother and wife, and you're amazed by her. You read about Priscilla and how she led a church with her husband, Aquila. You see mentioned by the Apostle Paul a great female apostle, a contemporary, Junia, and you think briefly how you would like to be able to impact your generation in that way. Then you quickly settle back into, *But who am I? I am just a woman.* And you think to yourself, *Those were exceptions.*

You read Bible scholars who wrote in their commentaries that God chose women like Deborah because there were no qualified men, and you shrink back into your comfortable place, thinking that you're not exceptional. You look around and see many qualified men. *Surely God has a role for women that does not involve leadership in His kingdom, leadership of His people*, you think to yourself.

You consider it again and again as you look around and see oppression, but then you come upon the Apostle Paul's words in his letter to his son in ministry, Timothy, in 1 Timothy 2:12-15: "I suffer not a woman to teach a man, not to usurp authority over him ..." And you shrink back again to do what you've always done.

But in this season, God is calling His daughters. He is calling his modern-day Miriams and Esthers, Huldahs, Deborahs, Priscillas, and Junias. He is calling His daughters out of the shadows of obscurity and into position on the spiritual battlefield for the souls of mankind, calling them to take the mountains and gates of government, entertainment, religion, education, media, arts, and business alongside their warrior brothers. I didn't realize it at the time, but I had fought a battle of the mind with my health that equipped me for a promise I had received many years before. The healer rose up.

You are in a battle now. What is the adversary that has come up against you, calling out in you as it opposes you? Rise up and answer the call!

The Spirit of Jabin

The spirit of Jabin is a spirit of intimidation and is usually the first enemy an emerging leader faces. Jabin was an oppressive Canaanite king who ruled in 1402 BC, from a dynasty of oppressive kings of the same name. He was noted to have had nine hundred chariots. He used his chariots as visual intimidation—psychological warfare—against his adversaries. And Sisera, the commander of his army, was his enforcer. The people of Israel were paralyzed by fear because of Jabin and Sisera. If any of those he conquered thought to rise up to get free of the oppression, the chariots were a reminder of his might and their lack and insignificance.

Most emerging leaders will face their own insecurity through the intimidation of an adversary or challenge. Intimidation becomes a teacher. The teacher reveals the insecurity. It shows us how we view ourselves as small and our enemy as greater and more significant. The teacher teaches us that our oppressor is too big for us. That knowledge will either paralyze us or cause us to rise up.

The oppressed people of Israel rose up. And in rising up, they called upon the One who is greater than all. If they were going to be free, they had to overcome the fear that intimidation causes, call upon God for help, and courageously obey His instructions when He answered. They called upon their God, and God raised up from among them a leader. Throughout the history of the judges of Israel, we see that the people would call out to God when they were oppressed, and He would listen to them in time and raise them up a judge as a leader to galvanize the people, give them courage through the word of the Lord, and remind them of who they were.

Deborah the judge and her military general, Barak, rallied and galvanized the people and raised a large army of men who were willing to rise up to face their oppressor at the encouragement of their leader, Deborah. She was confident in who she was and confident in Her God. She heard the word of promise over the people. It was a word of victory. She knew God to be a promise-keeper. She rose up, and her confidence inspired confidence in those around her.

The way to win against the spirit of intimidation is to have a healthy sense of your identity in Christ. Deborah was confident in her role as a judge. To judge at that time was to occupy an office. She was the first female judge in a time when women were not valued beyond producing heirs and workers. Her work as a judge would compare to that of the office of apostle. She set order in Israel. She made decrees. She set mighty ones in position. She was governmental. She was also a known and respected prophet, which means that she spoke for God, people recognized her words as His Word, and both men and women came to her.

We are told that she would sit under a tree and the people would come to her for judgment. She did this so that as she met with men, the meeting would be public. She left no room for accusation. Women in ministry as well as men would do well to recognize the wisdom in that and set healthy boundaries. It is unwise to meet to counsel someone of the opposite sex alone; it is best done with others present in the room or in a public space. How many great leaders has Satan tempted to fall into the trap of sexual misconduct, and how many have fallen prey? Countless ones.

Within the historical context, and even with our modern concept of the role of women in ministry, it is difficult to make sense of the story of Deborah. Why would God choose a woman to lead when He made man to be her covering and head? Some have tried to make sense of it by explaining that God chose her because there were no qualified men. That explanation falls short in light of the fact, borne out by Scripture, that God never chooses the qualified but qualifies the chosen. He often uses what mankind considers weak to show His strength. There were many men God could have chosen, but He chose Deborah. Our infinite God cannot be boxed in by finite intellectual boxes.

Deborah was married to a torchbearer, Lapidoth. His name indicates that he was a shining one, a forerunner, one who brought illumination and went before the people, but he was not chosen. Barak was a military leader and man of valor, but he was not chosen. An army of ten thousand men was raised, but none of them was chosen. God chose who He wanted. He chose a woman. And she answered the call and positioned herself to do His will.

The men were not weak in comparison to other men, but in comparison to God, all are weak. Lapidoth had to be a strong man to cover what God placed on His wife. He had to be strong because God chose Him to protect this gift He was giving to His people to bring liberation. God called Lapidoth too. Lapidoth's call was vital in the freeing of the captive people. But the call on his life was different.

Deborah could have shrunk back into obscurity, but at the call of God, she rose up. Intimidation came before her, but she remembered the word of God, and she called the people together. She rallied the mighty ones. Leaders in general, and women in particular, have to be willing to push past the opposition and resistance to link with others and activate the anointing to gather that which resides on the inside.

Often those who need you most will fight hardest against you. Every Nehemiah who goes to build will have a Sanballat and Tobias rise up to draw people away and resist the work of unification—some out of jealousy, some out of a fear of change, and others out of a rebellious spirit at operation in them. But whatever the root and cause, the resistance will come; and the resistance will make the leader who pushes forward against it stronger and more capable to lead.

When I was a teenager, the spirit of Jabin came up against me. I knew the call of God to ministry upon my life, but I was very shy. I was insecure and easily intimidated. I always felt that my words had no value and that no one wanted to hear my thoughts.

When I was eighteen, I received a word of promise about the prophetic call on my life. Happy to receive the word and even happier at the prospect of being viewed as significant, I set out to operate in the gift I heard was in me. I was "prophesying" to everyone, giving pathetic words. I remember once standing in a worship service and walking very slowly to the pulpit to deliver a "prophetic word." I walked slowly to look holy, and when I got to the pulpit, I stared at people for a while before I began talking so that I could look really deep. The "word" was very general and from the soulish realm.

When I think back now, I laugh at my naïveté, display of insecurity, and lack of knowledge of my identity. And I thank God for his grace that covered me and the ones who had to hear me while I was being processed. Anchoring the insecurity in my mind were the times when I would share my thoughts and the listener would cut me off. The enemy of my destiny wanted to silence me by making me feel insignificant—unseen and unheard.

Speaking and social interaction became giants for me. The giants discouraged me. I withdrew into a protective shell. I called the shell *introversion*. The enemy was setting a trap. He wanted to intimidate me so that I would shrink back in fear and not release the word God was putting in my mouth—the word of release to the captives. The captor hates the liberator and works vigorously against the liberation of his captives.

The word is always the target. To get to the word, the enemy will attack the word-bearer. The adversary will tear up the ground to get to the seed. The enemy, however, cannot succeed in stopping what Father God has purposed. As long as the earth remains, He has promised seedtime and harvest.

CHAPTER 2

Qualifications of a Leader:
The One God Calls, He Also Qualifies

Now Deborah, a prophetess …
—JUDGES 4:4

I am oil, and I am water. Some would say the things that make me who I am do not mix, but I see how Father God mixes them to make a beautiful iridescent picture.

I'm an African American female raised in rural Texas. I'm educated and drawn to academia. I am practical, and I am a woman of great faith. I like order and freedom of expression equally. I am Christian pastor—some would call me *evangelical*—but because I am a woman, many evangelicals would say I should not be allowed to pastor.

I am from a Wesleyan, Armenian, evangelical holiness background, very conservative, but some have labeled me charismatic or hyper-charismatic and liberal. I am a social conservative and a pro-lifer who doesn't agree with the death penalty and believes that global warming exists. I have strong convictions, but I love people deeply—even, and especially, those with different beliefs and convictions from my own.

When I ran for political office in the past, friends would not vote for me because I identified as a Democrat. To them, labels were more important than what they knew about me. I lived what they said they were voting for, while the ones they voted for spoke about it from a card of party speaking points while living something very different.

I'm an enigma to some and an anomaly to others because I cannot be stuffed neatly into a box. There is no box that will fit me, no label that will describe me. As leaders, and especially female leaders, we must be above labels, titles, boxes, and names. What we are called to do is bigger than a name.

While being a female in ministry has its share of challenges because of the box many create for women, being an African American female has added challenges. And an African American female pastor in rural America has to have true grit and confidence in her identity, because nonacceptance is great. If she is not careful, the nonacceptance and perceived or actual nonattainment can make her bitter, and she will begin to minister from her hurt and out of rejection. This is a peril of the ministry journey of many females.

But on the ministry journey, God protects His servants who are willing to allow Him lordship from taking on a spirit of rejection; while being processed by rejection, He prepares them for exploits that reflect the glory of the Kingdom rather than self-glory.

We Walk by Faith

I had been in ministry for twenty years and was praying about starting schools. I wanted to start a school for ministry—a ministry equipping center—and a classical Christian school for kindergarten through twelfth grade. I had served as a teacher for several years at our local high school and knew that I was a gifted teacher. I had a big vision but very few people resources and even fewer financial resources.

I was a risk-taker and a woman of great faith. I had often taken leaps of faith that others would have considered illogical. The irony is that I am a very practical person and like to plan, but I am also a woman who believes her God. If I hear Him call, like Peter, I will jump out of the boat, forgetting the waves.

I respected public education, but I had a heart to offer children an alternative to public school. Over the course of three years, I worked to start my schools. I had acquired a building that was too expansive, too expensive, and had too many structural issues to grow a ministry in. It had no insulation in the area we would use for a sanctuary, and on our opening service in September, it was 105 degrees inside. People stayed as long as they could for our first service, but one by one, the crowd—sweaty in the sweltering Texas heat—began to dwindle.

Each year we spent in that building frustrated me. It had great potential. I could see that it could house my vision, but without people and finances, we were handicapped and stuck in a holding pattern. The people we had were overworked, and as conflicts arose, those who had come would leave.

I knew I was to start a school. I knew I was in the right place. Perhaps, however, it wasn't the right time. Maybe I was doing something wrong. I could feel frustration starting to increase and the familiar heaviness of depression trying to come upon me.

One night after a particularly rough day of ministry work—ministering to those who were questioning and complaining—and emotional duress at the lack of resources to even pay the rent for the facility we were using, I cried myself to sleep after my husband prayed for me. I woke up early the next morning and went to my computer. I opened a message from Alexis, a young woman I had friended on social media but had never met in person. She began by writing that it didn't make sense to her what she was about to write, but she knew it was for me.

She continued, "The Lord would say to you, 'My plans for you have been straight since '98. The anointing upon you runs deep like the (flooded) Blanco river and no amount of educational attainment can equal what I have given you by my Spirit. You will see limbs restored. I see you mining by a gym and a school pops up.'"

Did she say a school pops up? I was flooded by emotion. I felt so enveloped by loved at that moment. My Father God saw me, saw my tears, and sent a word to encourage me.

The words resonated. I had heard similar words before, but I couldn't put my finger on the significance of "straight since '98." As I was pondering the words she wrote and trying to figure out the significance of 1998, I remembered my old journal. I wrote everything in that journal. I found it in a box in my closet after searching for a while. I read for a while, laughing at things that in those times seemed so significant, even daunting, though they were all panned out and seemed trivial. This encouraged me. It was going to be okay. It was already okay. My Father

God saw me. He called me. He gave me the desires that were in my heart. He would cause it to come to pass.

When I came to 1998 in my journal, I had to fight back tears. That was a very difficult year and a time of defining moments, with significant words of knowledge and wisdom. It was the year I was licensed as a minister of the Gospel and began an intensive ministry training program. It was the year I began work toward a masters in theology. It was the year I heard again a word that had been spoken over me by a little Nigerian prophetess in her living room when I was eighteen years old—a word that confirmed reoccurring dreams I'd had since I was eight.

The word I received in 1998 was again given in a living room—not in a formal religious setting but in a meeting of believers who were a part of a larger congregation, gathered for study and worship. Seeing me, the leader of the home group meeting, who had never met me, called me up to him and began to speak to me. As he spoke, the others gathered around me and began to pray and speak in turn words from the heart of the Father to my heart.

The leader, Brother Piuos, an American Nigerian prophet, began to speak as I knelt in the presence of God I felt in that place. He said, with his hands on my head, "God has given you a signs, wonders, miracles, and deliverance ministry. You will heal people. Your shadow will transfer the anointing. You will travel to countries to minister and people of all ages, backgrounds, nationalities, and ethnicities will be drawn to you. All your needs will be met even before you call to Him to have them met. You are named rightly, for whatever you tie will be tied and whatever you untie will be untied. You don't have to depend on knowledge, for what you receive from the anointing will be greater than what you receive from knowledge. People from all ages and all nationalities will be drawn to you. You will not have to wait a long period to see it; it will come suddenly. You will see limbs restored. You are a world changer."

I was in awe. Speechless. I felt awkward, because all I could do was weep. It had been a difficult year. Nothing seemed to be happening as I thought it would. Yet everything I had talked to Father about, He was addressing. I saw in my journal how I had asked in 1997 for a signs, wonders, and miracles ministry because I wanted to see people truly healed and set free. I didn't want to simply bandage them up; I wanted them to see the true power of God.

In 1998, a word had been given that confirmed that Father heard the desire of my heart. That was also the year when I first heard Father's voice audibly. I was startled. The sound seemed to come from all around me, engulfing me. It was like no sound I had ever heard before. It reminded me of the sound of crashing waves on a beach in its depth. "I have sanctified you for myself" were the words in the sound.

The weight and significance of the words didn't strike me immediately. I was young. I had believed in Jesus and received Him as my savior at age eight. I read stories of the Bible, and I loved the stories of the patriarchs, even praying that God would make me like one of them. I talked to him daily, but I had never heard His voice like this. It had always just been a knowing, or soft impression and prompting. But this was different. I heard Him with my ears, and His presence became more real to me.

What made the experience even more profound was that I was engaging in activity that I had been taught was sinful as a child. Hearing His words of acceptance and love while I was doing something that I had tried to overcome the desire for over many years was more than I could bear. I was undone. I sat and cried. I was taught that once you were saved, you didn't sin anymore. Consequently, I found myself locked into a pattern of self-condemnation, ritualistic repentance, and stumbling after walking for a few months in the power of my will to please God. I was legalistic and judgmental, and I tried to be perfect in my own ability in order to please a God who, though I was unaware, was already pleased and very deeply in love with me.

I later learned that it was by faith that I pleased Him, and everything that was not of faith was sin. I thought that if I could get everything perfectly right, I would be qualified to do what He called me to do. I had told Him in my private times of devotion that if He would take away the desire for this thing, I could be perfect. Little did I know that there were so many more things that He needed and wanted to correct and perfect in me and that if He revealed them all at once, I would be overwhelmed. I would come to understand later, as He continued to reveal His love for me, that although I was perfect positionally, I was on a journey toward perfection. I was flawed, but He spoke to me that day that despite my inability to please Him on my own, He called me. While I was still in sin, He loved me and set me apart for His own sacred use.

With those words, He let me know that I did not belong to the enemy, I belonged to Him. In order to set people free, I had to be free, and that was a moment of liberation that would be followed by many other liberating experiences in my life. I understood that I couldn't qualify myself. He qualified me. No experience, no educational attainment, no social status, pedigree, or prestigious ministry position would qualify me. Since the beginning, He chose those He desired to impact others, and He brought them into covenant relationship with Him. In choosing, He also qualified them—usually the ones who everyone else would have rejected.

Rejection, a Qualifier

Deborah would have been rejected from leading the people as a judge and prophet, but God's choice was undeniable, as His hand was upon her and His words were in her mouth. Her work spoke for her. And mighty ones, male and female, were drawn to her.

As a leader, and especially a female leader, you will experience rejection and nonacceptance. But God often uses rejection to qualify His leaders. Those you love most will sometimes love you the least. Those you are fighting for will sometimes fight against you. Some will lie about you. People lied about Jesus too. The servant is not greater than the master.

You've been betrayed, used, rejected. So was Jesus. He was acquainted with sorrow. As He was dying, the people He was dying for denied Him, left Him, spat upon Him, pierced Him, and mocked Him. Yet he responded, "Father, forgive them, they don't know what they're doing." He gave up His life, but He took it up again. And now, after passing every test, He is seated in power. He has outlived every lie, and everyone will speak the truth that He is King of Kings and Lord of Lords.

The enemy of your destiny desires that you take on a spirit of rejection with bitterness and unforgiveness in order to paralyze you. But God allows the rejection as a teacher to qualify you. Your challenge in the rejection is to not take on rejection—while being offended by an offender, to not take on offense. The way we pass this test of rejection as leaders is to refuse to give up on the hope of our calling, to refuse to let go of the word of promise over our lives. We remind ourselves of what God has said of us.

We remember that we are accepted by Him and loved unconditionally. We remember that we are fearfully and wonderfully made. We remember that we are the apple of His eye. We focus on Him as a prize. We choose not to focus on gaining the approval of man but rather on doing what we do as a freewill offering to God.

We refuse to get caught in the world's rat race, chasing titles and status and money. We refuse to get caught up in personal ministry kingdom-building and running numbers and filling stadiums to prove ourselves successful in ministry. We choose to submit to Him. We choose to follow His instruction, even if it means that we will be embarrassed or might fail, while being fully persuaded that we will not fail.

Everyone experiences failure, but how you respond to the failure—how you recover—speaks of the readiness of your character to be used to do great things. It can also be a jailer to your future, holding you captive, paralyzed, shackled by fear of future failure and loss. The Israelites had been defeated and taken captive by the Caananites who oppressed them. They had failed God. They failed their nation, they failed themselves. But even after failure, being heavily oppressed, they called out to God, and He heard them and sent a deliverer once again. He sent them Deborah. He raised her up as a prophet out of national failure. They had failed as a nation numerous times before, but in His faithfulness, God would hear and answer when they called. When the deliverer was made known, the people were willing to try again despite the fault of the past. Even though before them was the record of their failure, they were willing to hope again.

If you have experienced failure on the way to your promise, hope again. God will raise you up as a voice out of the place of failure. Be willing to get up and show up. Shake off the fear of failure and embarrassment and move toward the future goal, one foot in front of the other. Others are waiting for your voice and strength of leadership to call them out of their places of failure and disappointment.

Victory in Defeat

"I'm going to run for county judge!" I heard myself say as I sat up in bed. My husband had a look of surprise on his face, and I was more than a little surprised to hear myself say it. My husband had served as Bastrop County judge for fourteen years, after being elected at age twenty-seven as the youngest in Texas history in that office and the first African American to be elected as a county judge in Bastrop, He shared the latter honor with the judge elected at the same time to represent Travis County.

That the favor of the Lord rested on his life was very evident. He was a trailblazer, and victory seemed to come easy for him. Even in a rural area that still had hanging trees that had displayed hate for black bodies, Father gave him favor with man. In a county with less than 12 percent African American population, he was accepted, and he won the hearts of the people. He loved the county, and he loved the people. And they loved him.

But I had always had to fight for victories, and although I knew I had favor with Father, I didn't see the same favor with man. I knew this would be a different race from the ones my husband had run. Yet I also knew it was something I had to do.

My husband had retired after successfully leading our county through one of the largest fires in Texas history. I was with him when he first ran for office and for every election after that. I saw how emotionally and physically taxing public service was. I knew what the job entailed. That knowledge didn't inspire me, but the sense that I was supposed to run did. I knew that I was up against a giant of a challenge.

I am not as relational and charismatic as my husband, which was a challenge to electioneering, and Bastrop was a rural county that had only had one female judge of record, which presented an even bigger challenge. They were not used to women in upper levels of leadership. That judge had held a lower public office previously, allowing her to prove herself for an opportunity for a higher position. Men could see her doing the job because even though she was female, she was proven and had gained some trust.

Nonetheless, there were still many who simply would not vote for a woman for a top-level public office. Many felt women were too emotional to lead. I personally heard several express this sentiment. More challenging still was the fact that I was an African American female. Even those who knew me seemed to question whether I was suitable for that level of leadership. I was allowed to discern their thoughts, seeing past their smiles and through the nodding of the head as I spoke.

I had run for office before. I ran for school board against an incumbent and won. But I had been a schoolteacher. It was easier, I believe, for people to see me in that role. I was elected to the board of trustees and later by the other trustees as the first African American female president of the board. We were making progress, and those people were some of the best in the world, but we were still rural. The population of the county was exploding, but the percentage of African Americans in the county was not increasing.

And there were other challenges. I was the wife of the former judge, and there was an antiestablishment wind blowing at that time. (How we were thought of as establishment still baffles me.) But despite it all, I felt that for some reason, I was supposed to run. I stepped out on faith and ran the race. I represented the Kingdom of God well. I prayed. I believed. But I lost.

I was devastated. How could I lose? I knew God had prompted me to run. I was qualified. I had a passion for the well-being of the people. I cried all night and vowed I'd never run again unless Gabriel or Michael the Archangel appeared to me and commanded me to run. I was hurt. I was fatigued. I was embarrassed. I just wanted to hide out. But God had given me the gifts of resiliency and tenacity. I had experienced failure, loss, and embarrassment before, and each time, He gave me the strength to wash my face after crying all night and show up again the next day.

A few months later, I decided to pursue another office as a Texas state legislator that came open because a legislator stepped down to take a position elsewhere. I stepped out on faith. I struggled raising money. I have never liked asking for money. I grew up poor and proud. We didn't receive any government assistance, and I was taught to be excellent in all things, to pursue education and never to depend on anyone for anything. I still remember my mother instructing my brother and me when we went to visit others in our community, "Don't ask for anything!

Even if they offer, you refuse." And as a pastor, I understood that the public perception of pastors and ministry workers is often of one on the take who gets wealthy at the expense of parishioners by taking up large offerings.

The lack of financial resources was a challenge. I was also challenged in relationships. Through the campaign process, I discovered that some who I thought were with me as friends were not friends. Some were jealous of the life I was living that they thought was perfect. Some wanted to see me fail. Some questioned my motives. Some just didn't believe in me.

But as God was revealing hearts and purging and pruning my circle, He was also circumcising my heart. He was removing any residue of the Saul spirit—that people-pleasing spirit of compromise and insecurity. He was building me up through a process that appeared to be breaking me down. He often deconstructs to construct. He was forging me in fire to be a weapon in His hand.

I remember a gentleman who was politically connected, wealthy, and established—a kingmaker of sorts—telling me that signs and forums didn't win races. He explained that voters didn't vote on virtue or issues, but image. Money pays for an image. It was money that won, and whoever could get the most money and did what it took to get it and keep it had the power. Much to my chagrin, in many cases, I found what he said to be true.

There were those around me who advised me to do things that were politically acceptable but not acceptable for me. The powers that be had their way of doing things, but I answered to a greater power. I refused to compromise, because what I was doing, I was doing for my Father God. In the end, I would have to answer to Him for what I did and how I did what I did.

As I continued to campaign, Father continued to reveal … and to separate. There were those with me who, like the children of Israel in the wilderness, could not go with me into the promise, and I had to learn how to let go. I had to learn how to let go of the people and to let go of the pain. I learned how to trust God, love people deeply, and hold them loosely. I learned.

I lost that race. I remember when the results were read, I turned at once to the friends who had gathered, and my eyes were drawn to one who had been my friend since I had moved to Bastrop. I saw a slight grin on her face. I knew that she was trying to hide the fact that she was happy I lost, but her smile gave her true heart's meditations away. My heart was broken more by that than the election results.

I never told her what I saw. But my husband was there and held me, and I sunk into his chest, fatigued. Again, I was emotionally overwhelmed. I vowed again to never run again. This time, I was okay with not winning. I learned a lot of valuable lessons in the process. I was strengthened in some areas of weakness, and I was revealed to again about my true identity in Christ. I was made confident. I understood more than ever that as Christ was on the earth, so am I. And in Christ, even when it looks like we lose, we win.

Chasing Hope

There were many times over the years after I planted the first ministry in Bastrop that quitting was a thought almost monthly, but it was never an option. I knew that what I was doing was not a job but a calling. I couldn't quit, and I couldn't retire. All I could do was transition as He granted permission. I loved Him, and I lived to honor Him. I would not dishonor Him by quitting. And I was plain out stubborn. No matter how badly I wanted to quit, I would not.

I remember once, as a child, being spanked by my mother for disobedience. I stared at her and would not cry. She sent me to a place of isolation, but that didn't break me either, much to her chagrin. That and other tests proved that I had the strength of character to stand under pressure that God had developed in me even as a child. I was made for the fire—knitted together, formed, and fashioned to stand and to withstand attacks.

My personality, temperament, love language, birth order—everything was intentional and on purpose for His purposes. As I grew, God refined me in the fire I was made for and turned the stubbornness into tenacity. He made me a fiery minister, minister of flame. This was done to prepare me for what was ahead. All leaders have character-development tests designed to refine them to be able to stand under future pressure. Weapons are often refined by fire. And God's choice weapons are often refined seven times by the hottest fire.

Our ministry grew to a critical mass within the first year of ministry, and we had to move from a small building we affectionately called "the barn" into a larger one to accommodate the growth. When we transitioned into the new building, we continued to grow until we started doing deliverance ministry. The people in our region were not accustomed to this type of ministry, and we were novices. We allowed a lot of manifestations that caused fear in visitors. Our name was in the wind, but not in a good way. We attracted many with church hurt and with rejection, abandonment, and orphan spirits.

Because we were small enough for close interaction with all parishioners, many desired more time than I could give and would be offended and leave because I could not satisfy their longing—the longing that only Jesus could satisfy. Our ministry would surge and then decrease. Father used the times of decrease as a teacher. The teacher showed me my heart. Although I loved Father and wanted to honor Him and to advance His Kingdom by bringing people in and healing and equipping them, I also had at the same time a desire to fill seats in order to be seen as legitimate in ministry by my peers in ministry. I felt that many didn't consider my ministry valid and didn't think I could do the work. I wanted to prove them wrong, and my ministry had the stench of that fear of failure and people-pleasing on it.

In times of decrease, Father kept me. He showed what was in my heart so that he could correct it, so that He could straighten the bent that the lack of identity had made. At times, we had large tithers leave, but Father would have someone step up to fill the gap. Sometimes people from outside our fellowship would commit to give for a season, and we were sustained. In the times that the numbers would decrease, we would struggle and sometimes become anxious, but God sustained us.

He taught us in those years that He is our provider—that He was the builder of the ministry and that the ministry was His responsibility. He supernaturally sustained us and gave us favor, so much so that people we didn't know and some we had never met began to sow into our ministry so that our financial obligations were met. We never had to beg for bread.

Father prepared our hearts in those years to never compromise our ministry for the sake of tithers or charitable donations and not to concern ourselves with numbers and filling seats. Our responsibility was to fill hearts, and He would fill the seats as He chose and when He chose, for His Kingdom purposes. After five years of having our hands trained for war, we moved so that our fingers could learn to fight. We moved into a smaller building, and two years later, another small building.

Initially, it was embarrassing to me that we moved so often. It made us appear unstable. But later, I saw that each of the places we moved to was strategic. Each place was at a crossroads in the city or a major artery. Because of where we were situated, the warfare was intense in those places. I learned later that those who involve themselves in the occult often speak curses at crossroads and plant fetishes at those places to bring death and lack. We were put in those places to bring life where the enemy desired to bring death and poverty.

In one area we moved into, there were active Wiccan covens, and we could sense an adversarial presence there. It appeared to many that we were decreasing and that we would fail. Many ministries that started at the same time we did had already closed their doors. But I would not give up on what we knew God called us to. How could I? He never gave up on me.

I had many nights of crying into my pillow, feeling rejected by the ones I loved, the community I lived in, and my peers in ministry. But joy always came in the morning. I would get up, dry the tears, and show up again. I even told Father God in prayer once that I would never leave ministry, but I desired to leave the pastorate. I was going through the motions, doing what I had to do because I would not stop, but my heart was not in it. I felt depressed each time I drove into the parking lot of the church during those years. But I would worship until I saw Father high and lifted up and then stand to preach under His anointing.

Despite the way I was feeling, despite my inadequacy, He met the needs of the people through me. And He continued to bless us. We had family friends, relatives of my husband, the Browns, who gave us favor and allowed us to rent for a nominal amount a very nice space in which we could recover and regroup. They could have rented the space for double what they were charging us, but they favored us and were always present to help us when we were in need, even though they were not parishioners.

In that place of rest, Father spoke to my spirit by His Spirit to "Strengthen what remains!" I was crying even in the place of rest for the children who were lost and the ones who never were. But it was time to get up. I did so, and my husband and I began strengthening the core with training and development programs and seminars. We gave them assignments designed to equip them in every area of ministry function. Some true leaders and true sons and daughters emerged during that time.

After four years in that place of restoration and refreshing, the door was opened for another move—a big, giant-step-of-faith move. One night as I was praying, I asked about our next move, as I sensed it was time. I heard the words *warehouse on Highway* 95 in my spirit as I went to sleep. When I woke up the next morning, I told my husband what I heard as I prayed. He nodded but didn't engage me in conversation about it.

I drove up and down Highway 95 later that day, but I didn't see a building for rent or sale. Later that night, a pastor who operated heavily in the prophetic and word of knowledge, Pastor Draper, who we had only met once, called us after getting our number from a mutual friend in ministry. He talked to my husband first and described a dream he'd had. In the dream, he saw us moving into a warehouse on Highway 95. He said Father God told him to communicate to my husband that he was not to worry about the price of the building and that I was not to worry about chairs. He said I would not like the chairs, but Father was going to take care of the chairs.

After the conversation, my husband told me that he knew exactly where the building was. He hadn't mentioned it before because he knew it was too far outside of our price range. We both laughed at that. He was the practical one who kept me balanced, and I was the one who pushed him out of his comfort zone.

The next day, I called the real estate agent for the building my husband told me about and arranged a meeting. I sensed that the agent was more than an agent, and I heard *son* in my spirit. He was intelligent, well-spoken, and very nice, and he seemed to want to work with me. He informed me that many churches had inquired about the building, but the owners were not willing to lease to them. They wanted to sell. But the building had been on the market for a while, and they might be willing to lease. He asked me what we could lease it for.

I said a quick prayer for an amount and responded, "Five thousand dollars."

We couldn't afford five thousand, but I knew this was our building, and I knew my Father who had provided for us time after time over the years would do it again. We shook hands, and he took the proposal to the owners, who I found out later to be his parents. The owners agreed to allow us to rent a building that other ministries and businesses had tried to rent—prime real estate—but were not permitted. It had been hidden for us.

It was a beautiful building that had been a warehouse and manufacturing company in years past. The area that was large enough to use as a sanctuary had no air-conditioning or heat and no insulation—it was little more than a shed. The first two years there, I struggled to preach in the Texas heat that often rose in the springtime into triple-digit temperatures and remained in the triple digits well into winter. I would feel faint at times as I preached. The heat was intense. Many people visited and liked the ministry, but the heat was a hindrance to growth. In the winter, temperatures dropped dramatically and we could often see our breath as we sang, and we moved around a lot to keep our toes from freezing. Our praise became really exuberant during those months.

Because of the growth inhibitors, we struggled to pay our rent. But God gave us favor with the owner of the building for a season, and he extended us grace. One of our parishioners retired and offered to have the sanctuary insulated with some of the retirement funds. The church in which I grew up held fundraisers to purchase air-conditioning units for us. It was slowly coming together.

And Father God was supernaturally sustaining us. We received many words of promise while we were in the building that we would grow there and that we would not have to concern ourselves with insulation and air-conditioning and flooring or sound and acoustics. The promise in the words we received from prophetic people from around the globe was that God was going to make us say "Wow," and that the building would look like I saw it and desired it to be to reflect the glory of the Kingdom.

We received word that the building would be ours debt-free. I had dreams about the deed being mailed to us and felt in my spirit that despite the intense warfare, it would be worth it all. At the end of the fourth year in the building, our membership began to decline, and it became increasingly difficult to maintain. We fasted and prayed, believed and raised funds, but in the end, the owners decided to sell the facility, and we had to leave. I was disappointed. I was tired. We were homeless.

The ministries I was a part of before I planted the ministry in Bastrop had wilderness wanderings where they had to move from place to place. I saw their struggles having to move so often, and I did not want that for the ones I was to lead. But here we were, moving again. I discerned the thoughts of those who were around me and felt their disappointment. I knew their faith was hit hard. I didn't understand what was going on.

I knew God loved me, and I knew He had a plan. I just wished He would let me in on it. But I remembered the words of Job: "Though He slay me, yet will I trust in Him." And in my soul, I was settled with the assurance that whether I was on the mountain and everyone was celebrating me or in the valley where I was ridiculed and doubted, God was with me, and His love had never failed and would never fail. And I would praise Him all my days.

On Being a Woman in a Man's World

It's a man's world, but it wouldn't be
nothing without a woman or a girl.
—James Brown

I am an ordinary woman. I have an extraordinary call. The call of God is never for a specific gender or ethnicity but to one who will accept. Because of the fall of man and subsequent curse, it has become a man's world, but the Kingdom of God is not flesh and blood but spirit.

In the Kingdom, we are one. There is no male or female, Jew or Greek. There is no competition. Competition is a result of the curse. Man and woman were created to complement one another, but as a result of the curse that came with disobedience, the spirit of competition was allowed an entry point, and the woman was opened to a desire to overtake the man and the man a desire to subdue the woman when they were first commanded and given the authority to subdue the earth from which they were taken—to subdue not only the ground but their own bodies that were earthen, and the desires that were annually inside and good but, left unchecked and unsubdued, could be perverted and become deadly.

Because women are naturally strong influencers, motives have to be checked when it comes to position to be sure that influence does not become manipulation and the ability to complement does not become perverted into domination. Women have to be careful not to overtake and emasculate the men they are to work with to accomplish great things, and men have to be secure in their identity so they cannot be deceived into feeling threatened by the strength of the woman and start to compete with her, trying to intimidate her or hold her back. They must be careful not to subdue what they were created to speak life to, to cultivate and call forth into greatness.

The call on my life extended past ministry to the gates of education and government. I saw the resistance most clearly and felt it most strongly at the gate of government. The resistance was from women and men. There were women who would not, and told me so, ever support me in a position of authority because I was a woman. And there were men who would not support me because I was a woman. I have had women say to me, "I will not vote for a woman for that position." And I have had men call me "little lady" and "gal" while we talked about important issues in a way that let me know that I needed to stay in my place.

When I first ran for public office, it was for the Bastrop Independent School District Board of Trustees. I ran against an incumbent, and I won easily. I had been a popular teacher in the district for many years, and my husband was an elected official and person of prominence in the community.

When I ran for office the second time some years later, with the same influence and background, nothing had changed, but I found the process much more difficult. Perhaps it was easier this first time because the office I ran for was considered acceptable for women, or perhaps it was because I was accepted in the realm of education but could not be seen in a leadership position in government. Perhaps it was because I didn't match the stereotypes that many held about females in leadership, and I was perceived as too soft for the position.

There were some great women in governmental leadership in my region, but most were extroverts, type-A drivers, and I was not. There were also no African American women representing areas that were not traditionally and predominately African American in demographic composition. I would find that when I went out to a campaign event with my husband, I was not addressed—he was. Even questions about me would be addressed to him. I often felt condescended to, and the weight of nonacceptance became cumbersome.

I was determined, however, to be true to myself and not change to fit into the box that was made for me as a woman in government. I would not try to take on characteristics that would make men feel comfortable around me, as the seductress or consort or drinking partner who would spit and cuss with them. I was also determined not to fit into the box created for me as a woman in ministry. I was once told that I was "too pretty to be a preacher." I felt degraded by the comment, but realizing it was an attempt at a compliment, I smiled politely. The inference in the comment was that women went into ministry when they couldn't do something better.

I have been referred to as "easy on the eyes" in introductions. I don't mind being thought of as attractive by Western standards, but I want to be thought of as holy first. While I don't mind being "easy on the eyes," I had nothing to do with that; it was divine design and genetics. I wanted the word in me to be heard and not be veiled by outward appearance. Some who walked with me in ministry wanted me to play up appearance and image, while others advised that I downplay it. I knew that I couldn't allow myself to be tossed by opinions; if I did, I'd never get anywhere, and I wouldn't complete the assignment that my Father God entrusted to me.

I couldn't allow myself to be pulled apart by opinions of how a woman of the cloth should dress. Some would argue that a clerical robe was best and modest, while others would insist that robes were religious and would point me to trendy ripped jeans and screen-printed tees. "Wear a little makeup to enhance! You're too plain without it," some would say as they pulled, while others would call me Jezebel or even condemn me to Hell because of the shade of my lipstick, pulling me in the opposite direction.

I refused to be a wishbone. I decided that people-pleasing would not suit me well. I didn't look good in that shade. So I decided to wear what I felt would honor my Father God and made me feel at peace. There have been those who have made me feel uncomfortable being an attractive female in ministry, some knowingly, some unwittingly. I have had women judge harshly my hair and clothes, my shoes, my nails. I have been treated as eye candy without any consideration for the anointing in my life. I sensed while in the presence of some that they felt they were above me and would not receive me as an oracle of God. There could be a word in me for them, but they would not receive the word because they could not receive the vessel. To receive the prophet's reward, you must receive the prophet.

To some, I was a trophy wife whose calling was to stand in the shadows, seen but not heard. There were many men and women I met on ministry assignments who had come to accept women in ministry, but many more who refused to accept a woman in a position of headship in the church, and certainly not as a pastor or apostle. I had received wise counsel from a woman in ministry when I preached my first sermon. It helped me when I encountered those people, and it still rings in my ear today: "Never try to prove yourself to anyone, and never fight for a platform. Let your work speak, and let the Holy Spirit be your defense."

I am an ordinary woman called to do extraordinary things, and God would open the doors. He would lead me. He would give me His words to speak, and He would keep me. Ordinary women answering a call to do great things in ministry is not new. During what was called "the Second Great Awakening," hundreds of women of various ethnicities and denominations stepped up to preach and occupy positions of leadership in churches. Many of those leaders used Deborah as an example of a woman called by God to publicly speak and lead.

Methodist evangelist Phoebe Palmer wrote in defense of the call upon women to preach. There were also women of Jewish faith who stepped up to the call of God on their lives and worked to open doors for women in ministry. Regina Jonas was ordained as a rabbi in Berlin in 1935. She contended that the precedent was set by Deborah, and since Deborah was appointed by God and accepted by the men of her time, so could other women be chosen by God and accepted by their male peers.

Deborah's role was public and official. She was authorized to lead both in the heavenly realm by God and in the earthly realm by the men who looked to her for leadership. As a judge, she was governmental. As a prophet, she was a spiritual leader who revealed the heart of the Father as His spokesperson. She was apostolic before the female apostle Julia stepped onto the scene. She and other women have answered the call of God on their lives, and even though some have tried to write them out of history, God protected their legacy. Their stories have not only affected those in their time but are inspiring generations and giving girls and women alike something to emulate.

CHAPTER 3

Preparation of a Leader:
When Preparation and Opportunity Meet

I remember growing up at my grandmother's house before my parents moved out on their own after college. My grandmother was a hardworking single mother of eleven. She was beautiful and strong. Her name was Lillie, and she was a lily of the valley. Her husband was a military man and a rolling stone. After his service in the military, he would visit her and his children, but he didn't live with her. They never lived together after he returned from military service, but they also never divorced. Divorce was very uncommon in their community during that time.

With money my grandfather sent her while he was on tours of duty, my grandmother purchased an acre of land and had a house built. He would send her money here and there, and she would use what she had to and save the rest. From the little that she had, she helped others in the community in which she lived.

When I was growing up, everyone in our little community of four blocks affectionately called her "Mama Lillie." She was a mother to the community, and everyone recognized it. She was the first Deborah I met. I remember her as one who loved unconditionally, and she was proud of me. I loved spending time with her and listening to her stories.

My mother was Lillie's youngest child. She was born when my grandmother was fifty years old, and my grandmother was advanced in age with much wisdom by the time I was born. Although she'd only had an eighth-grade education, she was the wisest woman I knew, and she taught me to read and write and some of my earliest life lessons. In return, when I was older, I would take her to run errands and help her as much as I could. She was tough as nails.

My first year as a teacher, I was called to the office and informed that my grandmother had suffered a brain aneurysm and was not expected to live through the night. I rushed out to meet my husband, who was my fiancee at the time, so that he could drive me to the city where she lived. We got there in record time and found her fighting death for her life—and she won. She lived several years after that, getting to attend my wedding and see the birth of my first child before she passed away, and I was honored to give the eulogy at her funeral and preach for the first time to my family the message of love in Jesus.

My grandmother was a fighter and a way-maker. She was never licensed for ministry, but she was a minister. After purchasing her house, she supported and launched out many children and grandchildren, helping them to get a start. She was a builder. And she made a house a home; she made something good even where evil lurked.

She was proud of the house she bought. It was a small house. It was the type of house that those who were in poverty lived in during those times, but it was hers, and she kept it nice. She maintained the house and yard so well that people would drive by to admire her garden, and visitors would compliment her on how immaculate the house was.

Although the house was clean in the natural world, much had gone on in that house over the years that opened doors for demonic activity and made it unclean spiritually. I remember hiding under my blankets shivering from an unusual icy coldness. What made this exceptional was that it was happening in the Texas summer in a house without central air. I would often feel held down, unable to breath, like something was sitting on my chest, and I was unable to cry out. I was awake; it wasn't sleep paralysis. I would find out later what it was.

This continued until I learned that when I called out "Jesus," even if muffled, I would be freed. I would see shadowy figures and hear bumps in the night—mostly at night, but not always. At night, I would dream. The dreams were almost always about the rapture, of me preaching as I saw signs in the sky of the return of Christ, or of me running from or fighting demons. My experience was not psychological, it was spiritual—it was demonic. I was exposed to a new world, a different realm, the realm of the supernatural.

After exposure came experience. My first experience with the casting out of demons also came when I was young. I was a teenager, and my family and I were very involved in our local church. Late one evening, my mother received a phone call. The first lady of our church, Joann, and a few other ladies were going to the house of a young couple to pray for them, and they had discerned that they needed additional assistance from intercessors. So they called my mother to also pray. They went to the house to find that the young woman had been touched by what she believed to be her husband's hand, in a way that her husband often touched her, but when she turned over, she found that her husband was not in bed. The ladies engaged the demonic spirit that was touching the young woman, and it left. That story scared me but intrigued me more.

After I graduated from Texas A&M University, I moved to Austin and settled into a church that later trained me for ministry. That ministry was both apostolic and prophetic in its mandate and process. I was placed there strategically to sit under and learn from a prophet who was also a poet, professor, and homiletics award-winning preacher, with an apostle as her husband who had a mandate to build people—a CPA and pastor.

Part of the credentialing and ministry-training process at that church was training in deliverance ministry. All the ministers in training were tasked with reading books and manuals on deliverance. I was required to read *Pigs in the Parlor* by Franck Hammond and books by Francis McNutt. Reading those books only whetted my appetite—what was to become a voracious appetite—for information about the ministry of deliverance.

I remember reading and realizing that I had deliverance issues. I needed deliverance! How could this be? I had been a believer since age nine. I was baptized at twelve and served in my childhood church from my teen years. I was assistant pastor in my current church. I loved God. And although I had many struggles and was keenly aware of my shortcomings, bents, and proclivities, I could not reconcile in my mind how the Holy Spirit could inhabit an unclean place with demons. But it was so. Anyplace in the soul that remains unyielded to the Holy Spirit can be occupied by a demon spirit, and the demon will oppress and torment its host.

I realized I had been oppressed by spirits of rejection, self-hatred, fear of abandonment, and others. I wanted to be free. I looked into the mirror and began to attempt self-deliverance. By the grace of God—because I had no idea what I was doing—some of the spirits were actually expelled.

I remember getting rid of things from my house that I felt would open up demonic portals. I laugh when I think about how the little Santa Claus decoration terrorized me. I was convinced its eyes were following me and it was possessed by a demon. I was unlearned, untrained, a novice … but that was changing.

After training in ministry for four years, I was ordained. After ordination, my pastors launched me out to begin a new work I felt called to build in Bastrop, Texas. They confirmed the call to launch out and blessed me. After seeking instruction from the Lord in prayer, I received the name New Life Fellowship for the ministry work in Bastrop. And in that name, our mission for a season was given. We were called to introduce people of religion to fresh, new, supernatural, peculiar life in Christ and deep fellowship beyond religion.

We didn't know what we were in for. We had no idea how massive this giant, this spirit of religion, was. We were called to a people and a place, and we were given a spiritual assignment to establish a ministry that would break up the stronghold of the spirit of bigotry, poverty, and division that often manifested as denominationalism, sectarianism, and racism in our area.

In 2001, I launched the ministry New Life Fellowship with three members: my mother, my husband, and my daughter. In 2002, we held our first formal worship service with thirty people in attendance. I had no bylaws, no five-year plan, no core group. I only had a statement of vision containing the mandate I felt God had given me for the region, and paperwork filed with the secretary of state and comptroller to make us official in the state of Texas. We didn't have a building to meet in until a few weeks before we launched, but God was faithful, and not only did we find a building, we were also blessed with pews from another ministry, and my mother purchased a lot of decorations to make our tiny little space look befitting a King. We didn't have much help, but I sense that was also strategic; when the word of God came to pass, no one could claim that they did it, but according to the word in Psalm 127 that was spoken over me in 1998, all would say, "The Lord has done great things for them!"

Holding my six-month-old daughter, I led worship, changing out transparencies with song lyrics while my husband changed out CDs on our little CD player. During offering and meet-and-greet times, I would feed my daughter and then come back in to preach and afterward minister at the altar. This became my practice for the next few months until God sent us consistent help.

I could see then in part why so many people were opposed to women in senior leadership in churches. It was very challenging, both physically and emotionally. My husband was my biggest supporter in ministry. He pushed me and encouraged me. His arms and prayers were a source of strength, and because he was confident in his identity, the talk he often heard from those who questioned my call to pulpit ministry didn't move him. He defended me and promoted me.

When men would insinuate that he had to have been weak for God to have chosen to use me, and when they asked how he could be head of our home and not head of our ministry, he didn't talk of himself and all of his accomplishments; he only talked of what he had seen and heard that made him confident of my call and election. He was as supportive as he could be, but as I was launching the ministry, he was launching his run for a second term as Bastrop County judge. He was away campaigning a lot. I was doing ministry, supporting him in his campaign, and raising a daughter. It was a challenge. But God was teaching me lessons about priorities and balance.

Leviathan

One day, as I was lying prostrate praying in our facility, as was my custom, I felt the push to look up at the ceiling. Looking up, I saw the word *LEVIATHAN*. After I looked, I sensed the Lord speak to my spirit: "The spirit Leviathan has come up against you." I heard that clearly. But although I had training in demonology, I didn't know much about this prince—or any principalities, for that matter.

When I got home from prayer, I poured myself into research about this Leviathan spirit of which Father God made me aware. I gained much knowledge, but it was without wisdom. I could recognize the attack of Leviathan upon our ministry for years after that and its devastating effects, but it took me many years and some casualties in war to learn how to effectively fight against Leviathan.

I learned that even in His name, there was a key to the strategy of Leviathan's operation against Levi, the priestly house. He was a fallen angel, a serpentine water spirit with many heads. His major assignment was against the priests and priestly houses—those who represent God to the people.

I also considered the second part of his name: Athan. *Athan* brought to my mind thoughts of the city of Athens. Athens was a center of knowledge and information, of human wisdom. Aha! This spirit, this principality, who was coming up against us was an information-gathering, prideful spirit, a perverter of vision and information and breaker of communication. He was a high-ranking spirit. He gathered intel about weaknesses and proclivities and attacked in those areas, consistently stabbing in areas of weakness so that they never developed into strengths and the organism was left lifeless and without blood, which represented power and strength for life.

He was doing that to us, and I was watching it as an observer who did not know enough to intervene. But in watching and applying what I read and saw in the book of Job, I learned that only God can hook the nose and control that monster, so I had to rest in Him. Although warfare, prayers, tongues, shofar sounding, and other weapons would break his works, only Father God could rout him.

I also learned that God gave us a part—and authority and power to do our part. Our part was to confront the adversary and communicate with our allies. We were to confront issues of strife, discord, division, whispering, competition, and sedition in the ministry in all its forms and also ensure proper communication at all levels. The enemy Leviathan hated conversation that opened up effective communication. He hated light being brought and clarity coming through communication. He worked to isolate members of groups through offense. And offended ones came together around their offense.

Leviathan was a water-like spirit. As water causes a distortion, impairing speech and vision and causing heaviness, so does Leviathan. He caused people who would work as great complementary team members to look at each other with suspicion or jealousy. He worked through offenses and intimidation to hinder their communication, keeping them from getting to the heart of the matter to gain understanding. An offended brother is harder to win than a fortified city. The enemy, Leviathan, knows this and will use the simplest, seemingly most insignificant things to bring destruction—a feather to cause a mountain to break.

Succubi

After five years of ministry, at one of our Wednesday night Bible studies, a young lady who had been attending regularly came up for prayer toward the end of worship. Although we had ministered deliverance, it had been infrequent. This was the night that we were thrust into the deliverance ministry at a higher level. It was a trial by fire—a sink-or-swim situation where all of the lessons learned over thirty years converged suddenly and all the information from books would have to be applied, but by the leading of the Holy Spirit.

The young lady was a believer. She was a prayer intercessor and gifted in the prophetic and in dance and music. She served faithfully in our ministry and was loyal. She became an unofficial armor-bearer and intercessor, and I loved her like a daughter. But she was heavily oppressed, and she knew it. She felt that something was about to happen when she came up for prayer, and she suggested that we all anoint ourselves.

I quickly organized a team and started praying for her, and demons started to manifest. One by one, the members of the congregation began to leave as the warfare became more intense, until I was left with a team of about twelve. We engaged the enemy all night, from about eight o'clock until five in the morning. There were times when we couldn't tell if we were talking to her or to a demon. At times, demons took control of her vocal cords and spoke through her. The voice that spoke was undeniably not her own.

One particular demon I engaged, I remember distinctly. As I called it out, it spoke back and told me I was tired.

"Liar!" I responded. I was not, but I knew many of my team were. I was irritated by it and made bold by the Holy Spirit. I answered, "This is what I was born to do!"

Yet it persisted. "You're not tired, but your team is," he said mockingly.

That was true. We had been there all night, but in my zeal and stubborn tenacity, I was not going to stop. I asked it what its name was.

"Ask your Father," it replied sarcastically.

It was silly to respond in that way. Hearing him say something I knew to be true—that God was my Father and I could ask—just made me even bolder!

"In the name of Jesus, what is your name?" I asked again.

It answered in a scratchy low voice, almost a whisper, "Sucubbi."

It was a succubus spirit, and there were more than one. Later, I understood why this grouping seemed to be more tenacious than the ones I had cast out earlier. It was a sexual demon that entered through the door of sexual perversion. Demons of sexuality and of the occult are especially stubborn because they affect not only the soul realm but the tripartite man—soul, body, and spirit—and they usually involve or result from deep trauma, often from early childhood.

Later, I realized that the demons I dealt with on that night were very strategic. Their plan was to tire me out, to drain me. Some demons, like rejection and succubi, were ones I had been introduced to as a child, and they wanted to overtake me. Although I felt powerful and secure in my relationship with the Father, I was drained.

I learned a lot that night. After many manifestations, and over a hundred spirits called out, I learned that the lists and instructions in the books and manuals are good for exposure and to lay a foundation, but they are not exhaustive and cannot be relied upon. The ear has to be open to hear the instruction of Holy Spirit. He is reliable. Revelation has to be fresh.

I learned to not talk to the demons and also not to depend on what I saw or heard—to not lean to my understanding. I was a novice, fascinated, and in my naiveté I spent time talking to and gathering information from liars, when I only needed to talk my Father and receive truth from His Spirit. Instead of going to books for answers and getting secondhand information, I could go to the Source (My Father) and his Word (the Bible) and get my "bread," my revelation, fresh.

Deliverance

One of the few times I see Jesus talking to demons in Scripture is in the case of the *Gaderene demoniac*. Any information gained from demons is secret knowledge and should not be sought out. Getting information from demons is a slippery slope that can lead into a dark place. In that instance, Jesus did not hold a conversation. He asked the man his name, and the gatekeeper demon replied, "Legion, for we are many."

Everywhere Jesus went, deliverance and healing took place. Deliverance is the children's bread, He said. And in Matthew 12:28, He said, "If by the Spirit I drive out demons, then the Kingdom of God has come to you." The Kingdom has come.

When Paul was preaching, a girl possessed by a demon of divination kept interrupting him. He didn't spend a long time with her casting out demons. He told the demon to leave, and it did. He didn't go look for the demon, picking a fight. He was on his assignment, and the demons came to interrupt. He was a carrier of the Divine Presence, and the demons had to manifest and then yield.

I understood that it was never about me or what I could do; it was always about Him and what He would do through me as I yielded to Him. It didn't have to take all night. It didn't have to be that complicated.

God spoke to my spirit that there was a certain measure of deliverance that should take place in the corporate worship (although some deliverance would still have to take place within the environment of a deliverance session with an individual). The problem is that much of what we call worship is actually performance, ritual, and empty defiled religion, devoid of the Divine Presence. We have smoke machines to replace the cloud of glory, the Shekinah; we have bright lights to replace the bright glory that should be on us. Performance draws and entertains, but Presence gathers and transforms. It is the Presence that routes demons. It is love that activates the power of the Presence.

Once, I had the father of a young adult bring his son to me. Demons were manifesting through his son, and the father was visibly shaken. I'd had previous encounters with both the son and the father. The son had attended our worship services, and we had cast out some demons, but by this time, I was tired of people experiencing the power of God in deliverance only to go back into what they were in and become worse, as illustrated in Luke 11:24—and afterward, in a worse state, come back to me again for another deliverance.

I didn't want to counsel him. I knew that demons can't be counseled; they have to be exposed and canceled. And then inner healing, counseling, and discipleship follow. I was tired of the spiritual backlash against myself and my family when I engaged in deliverance. His father didn't believe that I should preach or function in ministry as a woman; yet there they were, at my home.

As I headed to the door, it was flung open. I felt the cold, chilling presence of pure evil I had felt so often as a child. I knew what I was dealing with.

I was alone with my children. My husband, who functions in word of knowledge and discerning of spirits and usually works with me in deliverance and covers me, was out of town. The father was part of a denomination that did not accept women in ministry, and I knew he had never accepted me as a minister while he attended the church I pastored. He desired that his son attend somewhere else, but in desperation, he brought the young man to me. He spoke for his son, and I saw the desperation and love in his eyes.

He said that he was on his way to take his son to a mental hospital but knew that they would not be able to help him. They couldn't, but God did that night. Whether he walked in his deliverance after that or not I am not sure, but the love of Father God was evident and palpable that night.

I have seen small women punch holes through walls. I've seen men take on superhuman strength. I've seen faces contort and eyes turn serpentine. I've heard people growl like lions and slither like snakes. I've smelled the sulphur-like and hospital stench of demonic presence. I've seen spirits leave quietly with the fluttering of the eyes, no drama, or with a yawn or cough. I have also seen them leave violently, with vomiting and other manifestations. However they left, and wherever they went, it was always by the finger of God. I and my team were only vessels through which His virtue could flow.

Seeing these things, I was forever changed—strengthened in my faith. His virtue flows best through holy vessels, vessels without contamination. So self-examination, confession, and repentance are important in the lives of all believers, most especially in those who would function in deliverance. We were made perfect positionally at the time we became a new creation at conversion, but we are imperfect personally. We are being made perfect daily and strive toward future perfection. We must judge ourselves. We must keep our hearts pure before God. We must walk in love.

Once as I was preaching, in the middle of a sermon, I felt overwhelmed by love for a woman in the congregation. I'm a Navi and usually flow in the Spirit and the word bubbles up and out, and distractions can hinder the flow and frustrate me. But this was a divine distraction. I couldn't keep preaching. I felt such a deep love for her, the Father's love, that I became weepy. I called her up, and she shyly approached. She had been attending the worship services and serving humbly for over a year and had been prayed for many times. This time, however, God was going to do something different in the prayer.

When she came up, I was led to just embrace her. Afterward, I began to pray. I felt love mingle with that familiar boldness of the Holy Spirit, and I heard "rejection." I told her to look at me, and I commanded that spirit to leave. She began to expel through vomiting. I heard also "word curses by the father," so I broke those by the command in Jesus's name. My husband spoke to me other names, and we called them out. In ten minutes or less, the work was complete. Joy covered her. She began to dance around and worship. Love is the key that unlocks the power of the Presence.

Overcoming Demonic Oppression

Many believers know that demons exist but are ignorant as to how they operate and ignorant to our authority over them. Some do not believe that those in the Kingdom of God can be oppressed by demons. Perpetually sick, impoverished, accident-prone, vagabonds, proud, uncontrollably lustful, unable to achieve goals, unable to love, they blame other factors. "How can the Holy Spirit dwell in an unclean temple?" they ask. But many, many believers are unknowingly under the influence of demonic spirits and under demonic oppression.

Not every sin is from demonic influence. Some things are chemical, some psychological, some a result of us just being fleshly and responding from our flesh, our lust unchecked. But much of what we deal with in terms of the perpetual, the uncontrollable, and the insatiable is demonic. We are tripartite. We are spirit, soul, and body. The Holy Spirit's dwelling within our temple is within our spirit, spirit to spirit, deep to deep. The spirit of God made alive again our spirit so that we could commune again with God.

Our spirit, made alive and in-dwelt by the Spirit of God cannot be possessed by a demon; therefore, a believer cannot be possessed by a demon (Judas is a discussion for another time). But our soul (will, emotions, intellect, imagination) can be affected—oppressed by the devil. And oppression can feel like possession.

A believer can be oppressed by demons. The open door for demonic oppression is often trauma—fragmentation of the soul. Healing and restoration go hand in hand with deliverance. There are also doors opened by forefathers, and by sin and willful continued disobedience or breaking of a spiritual law. The kingdom of darkness is real. It has not gone away. But the kingdom of light is also real, and it too will never go away.

Many nonbelievers do not believe that demons exist. And because of some of the flakiness demonstrated in the Kingdom of God as it relates to deliverance—and many counterfeit ministers, false prophets, and lying signs and wonders—their unbelief is understandable. Their unbelief, however, cannot make demons unreal. They exist. And their agenda is to hinder the plan of God.

Demons hate humans, even the ones who are open to be used by them and those who worship them as gods. They hate what God loves. And they fear nothing—except God. They know Him, and they tremble before Him. They fear what is in God.

When we are hidden in Him and understand who we are in Him, demons tremble. When we walk into a room, full of His Presence, they cry out! And to the authority we have been given, they must submit. A believer who has been revealed to about demons' identity is a serious threat to the kingdom of darkness. "And these signs shall follow (or accompany) those who believe: they shall cast out demons" (Mark 16:17).

I am not special. All believers can and should cast out demons. We don't go looking for them; we just go about the Father's business, completing our assignment. But they will come, and when they do, we must stand in the power of the Holy Spirit. There will be those you love who will need deliverance. Do not be intimidated. God will send His angels to help. He will give you instructions. Follow His instructions. His Spirit will guide you into all truth.

He will send you teachers to train you. Some of your teachers will be people more experienced than yourself; other teachers will be situations and trials. Trust that God is the one who causes it to be. Whom the Son sets free is free indeed! All believers can and should function in deliverance; however, there are some who God has gifted and anointed to function more regularly in that ministry. For example, those called to the office of evangelist often have a special grace to function in deliverance. They may operate in gifts of discerning of spirits and the revelation gifts. Those in apostolic positions are often graced with anointing for deliverance, as the sign of an apostle is the working of miracles and signs and wonders accompany them, confirming the Word.

Deliverance is a sign that the Kingdom is among us. Those who are graced for operation at greater levels in this ministry often experience greater levels of opposition, retaliation, and backlash. It is not glamorous. The minister needs to be rooted and grounded in the Word and committed to consistent worship and times of intimacy with the Father, as well as a commitment to living a lifestyle of holiness and a tenacity and perseverance—a dogged determination to never, never, never give up. The enemy will allow a platform in order to work to make you fall from the platform for all to see, casting doubt on the power of God to keep what is committed to Him, to finish what He starts, to love. In all we do as ministers, as people of God, whether it is disciplining, healing, or deliverance, let us do it out of love, for the King and for the Kingdom.

CHAPTER 4

When the Word Tarries: On Being Stuck

"My plans for you have been straight since '98."

Out of all the words written in the prophetic message of encouragement sent to me by a stranger that day, those nine words seemed to jump off the page. The date given was seemingly random, yet it was significant to me.

What was significant about 1998?, I asked myself. It was 2016, and I had been in a time of intense spiritual warfare, emotional duress, and struggle for the past seven years. I had enjoyed periods of release and exhilaration only to go back to struggle, rejection, and heaviness.

The struggle, rejection, and heaviness always originated around ministry but would affect me personally, even to the point of physical fatigue and illness. My children saw the fight. They saw my husband and me pour into people, sometimes even leaving the children to sit and wait with my mother while we counseled hurting people or cast out demons or left in the middle of the night to console someone grieving. There were times when they did not receive things they wanted as children or needed as students because we gave what we had to those who came to us for ministry, only to have those people we poured our lives into leave the ministry saying we were not there for them or otherwise criticizing our communication, our service, or our ministry priorities.

I didn't want my children to resent the ministry and reject Church, as I had seen so many pastor's kids do, but what was I to do? I prayed for wisdom, for balance, and for skill in equipping them as pastor's kids, but I often felt inadequate and had a fear of failing them and failing the ministry—failing God.

But I am a fighter. I was bent on being the best mom I could be and steward the gifts God had blessed me with in them. I would not stop ministry. I had a mandate from God to preach, to minister deliverance and hope, to train and equip the Body of Christ for victory in war, and to train a travailing church in how to prevail. Often rejected by those in my own Church affiliation, at times I felt like an outsider, but my love for the Church remained.

Many times, I was not accepted because of my gender. Yet my love for the people—even the men and women who would reject ministry through a woman—remained. Often I was condescended to because of my ethnicity, but the distance caused by racial divide led me to long for racial reconciliation. I was often judged ineffective by ministry peers who had been given larger congregations and unaccepted because of the revolving door and relatively small size of our ministry. But God shifted my paradigm so that I neither despised numerical growth nor thought any longer of it as a measure of success. Instead, God placed in me a heart to build the Kingdom of God—to fill seats in order to fill hearts.

Rather than focus on the ministry Father called me to pioneer and then shepherd for fourteen years, I turned toward Kingdom expansion. I began to see the local fellowship I pastored as a place of preparation to train warriors to advance the Kingdom. God created in me a heart of deep love for the Church. She was beautiful in my eyes, even with all of her scars and flaws. I wanted to start a school—an equipping center for ministers. I wanted also to start a school for Christian children who wanted an alternative to public school.

For several years, the battle was intense. The local fellowship was experiencing financial hardship, and although my husband was very successful and well compensated financially in his work—a great financial manager and a tither with a generous heart—we could not seem to make ends meet. Every time we would get up, a financial whirlwind would blow in to knock us down and blow away what was in our hands; whether hospital bills from serious illness or an increase in property tax and mortgage, there was always something. We were embarrassed to the point that we couldn't be embarrassed any longer.

A prominent man in our community, my husband struggled with the knowledge that our financial hardship would be seen as a lack of integrity and character as we struggled to pay bills on time and keep our checking accounts balanced. There were times when we had to put groceries back at the checkout because cards were declined. There were times when we sat down to eat and then watched and wriggled in our seats and quietly prayed like we'd never prayed before for favor as we watched the waiter scan our card several times, returning to tell us our card was declined.

To compound matters, the gift of discernment was increasing in me, and I would hear the thoughts of those we served thinking that we were living off their tithe, offering, and ministry gifts. They didn't want to give in the offerings because they didn't want to give to us. I smiled hearing what they were thinking and kept loving and serving. My service was to my King, and they would be blessed as a result.

In these dark times of depression, disappointment, rejection, and embarrassment, I experienced the love of the Father in undeniable, incredible ways. Even in the struggle, we saw God's favor, as we avoided repossessions of vehicles when the ones sent to repossess refused to do so; instead, they gave us information so that we could reverse the situation. When we couldn't pay for food, managers would cover us, and we ate for free. I recognized the favor of God in our struggles, in our wilderness.

While we were being trained and our character developed to be containers of His glory, He kept us and showed us His glory. Daily He winked at us. But even though the Father continued to wink at us in the wilderness, showing us His love, I was in a place emotionally where I thought I was going to break if I did not get a break. I needed to hear something good from God. One word, and I would be okay. One word, and I would scale a wall and burst through a troop, but He was quiet and still.

I had a fire and passion for ministry that could not be put out, but I needed a fresh wind. I needed something to spark hope for greater, so that I would not settle in the place of transition and complacency. I was a fighter. I wouldn't give up. I would not stop, but I felt as though I was going through the motions in ministry, without life. I needed my joy back.

World-Changer

I hurried to my closet to grab a journal I had been keeping since 1995, sure that there was something written there that would give me a key to unlock hope again. I picked up the journal, and as I began to read, my eyes filled with tears. What I read restored my soul. There was a message there for me—words of encouragement and prophecy given in 1998 that seemed to have been delayed. It was now 2015, yet the word had not come to pass. But as I read the journal that chronicled words of knowledge, words of wisdom, words of encouragement, as well as tests and triumphs over the course of my life—not just the span from 1995 to 2005 that I was expecting, but from my earliest memories as a child and defining moments with God in early life to my present place—I could see God's grace and his hand painting on His cosmic canvas a beautiful work of art as the dark and light colors of my life and times converged, the sum of my experiences, good and bad, came together. I could see that though the words I held in my heart were delayed, I had been in a time of preparation for the fulfillment of the words in my life and that words were being fulfilled along the way in the most unexpected, supernatural ways.

The word from my journal written in 1998 was given first in 1989 when I was eighteen years old by a Nigerian prophetess, Bola, in her home. My mother had befriended her a few months earlier and wanted me to meet her. Bola was a very gentle, unassuming woman. She laughed and talked with us. After we visited for a while, she began to sing a song derived from Isaiah 60: "Arise, shine for thy light has come. Arise, shine for thy light has come. And the glory of the Lord has risen, the glory of the Lord has risen upon you."

After singing a verse, she said in a warm voice with a strong Nigerian accent, "The Lord says that He has raised up in you a prophet, and I praise Him that He has raised up in you a prophet for our day. The Lord says that you are like Deborah. Study her. Psalm 127 shall be yours, and Amos 9:13. God has given you a signs and wonders and deliverance ministry. He will heal people through you. Your shadow will transfer the anointing, and you will see limbs restored. People of all ages and all nationalities will be drawn to you. And all your needs will be supplied before you need them. You are named rightly, for whatever you tie will be tied and whatever you untie will be untied. You don't have to depend on knowledge. I will give to you by my anointing. You won't have to wait a long period; it will come suddenly. You are a world changer."

Tears ran uncontrollably down my face as she spoke. I felt encompassed by love. I hid the words in my heart.

As a child, I had been very insecure and shy. I didn't see anything great in myself. At fifteen, the first lady of my church came and sat near me after a worship service as I sat on a bench outside alone waiting for the rest of my family. She sat for a while and then looked at me and said, "I see greatness in you." Those words went to the core of who I was and ignited a spark in me. I hid her words in my heart.

In 1998, I visited my mother, who was living in Arlington, Texas. We went together to her cell group study. When we got there, the leader of the home group, Pastor Pious, told me to come to him, and the others gathered around. There were those of different ethnicities there and different cultural backgrounds. Pastor Pious was Nigerian. He began to pray for me as I knelt in the circle, and then he began to prophesy by the Spirit of God many of the same things that had been spoken over me in 1989 at Bola's house. He spoke a part, and then others started to speak, until all the words that had been spoken in 1989 were confirmed. Afterward, some were added. I was undone.

These words, this confirmation, came at just the right time. It was a time of struggle, and I needed to remember the word. I needed to focus on the healer and not on what needed healing. I had learned from the first time the word was spoken that it might not come as quickly as I would like, but God had a plan, and He was working it out. He was in control.

I felt the same excitement I had as a teenager when I first received the word rise up in me again. But the words were to be sealed in my heart for another time. As a teen, armed with a word, I was excited and ready to go change the world. As a child, I had been very timid. I didn't speak often, didn't really fit in at school or anywhere else and always felt as though I was on the outside looking in at life. I poured myself into books. Reading the Encyclopedia Brittanica—a set that my uncle brought us back home when he returned from the war in Korea—was my hobby, and my passion was reading the hero stories of the Bible and superhero stories of Stan Lee's Marvel Comics. I wanted to be Professor X, the powerful mutant telepath who trained other mutants to use their powers. I would pretend to be him.

I would pray to be like Moses or one of the patriarchs. I wanted to do great things. I wanted to help in big ways. I thought I was ready. I wasn't. But with that word, I was propelled into the place of greater preparation. The Lord said, "Study Deborah." And so study Deborah I did. He said He was raising me up as a prophet, so I began to try to act like a prophet. I remember squinting my eyes when I spoke to try to seem deeply spiritual. I remember trying to give people words, most of which the Lord did not speak. I was manufacturing them from my soulish realm. Then I read a word about how the prophet who speaks presumptuously would surely die, and I didn't want to die, so I stopped speaking.

I made an internal vow to never say "thus saith the Lord" and only to pray what I heard from the Holy Spirit to my spirit or to just say what I was hearing as if it were my words. This was good training for me, although still off-balance, because I was in a place of an extreme. I had so many insecurities and was so socially awkward that I was trying to prophesy to somehow gain respect, to be noticed, where I had always felt invisible before—to offer something where I had felt I had nothing to offer.

God began to speak to me about my identity in Him and about how much He loved me. As a child, I had reoccurring dreams about standing on the corners of streets and on highways preaching, about seeing the signs of the Lord's return in the sky, about the catching away, about fights with demons. I also had a reoccurring dream about the car of a relative. In the dream, I would run from window to window in my grandmother's house trying to get away, but every time I would get to a window, his car would appear. I knew, instinctively, that the car represented relationship and that I had tried to escape a traumatizing relationship, most likely sexual in nature, but was unable to escape.

As a young adult, I understood that someone in or close to my family had done something very harmful to me—had illegally touched me sexually, molested me, awakening sexuality before its time—but I couldn't remember who. I only had the detail of the car I saw in the dream. I knew the car belonged to someone familiar. This was significant, because as a child and a teen, I struggled with strong sexual urges unnatural for a child. I remained a virgin and by the grace of God, my husband was my only sexual relationship. As a child, I kept the urges secret, but I struggled and was ashamed. I carried a lot of guilt, and as I look back in retrospect, I understand that the insecurities and social awkwardness I carried were birthed during that time.

People would often say to me when I told them about how shy and insecure I was and that I thought I was ugly and stupid and that no one would ever want to hear what I had to say, that they couldn't believe that I would ever have that level of insecurity or could think I was ugly. But I did. Through the years, as I grew in fellowship with Jesus and became confident in my identity in Christ, I was set free from spirits of rejection, timidity, and insecurity. Out of the struggle, I gained spiritual strength and a message of hope and deliverance for others.

As a teen, as puberty in adolescence set in, the struggle intensified. The enemy used something natural and a seed he had planted in my early childhood to attack me. My parents were strong Christians and very protective. I didn't date. I had one male friend in high school, my pastor's son, with whom I was allowed to go to various functions. My parents trusted him somewhat because they knew his upbringing and because they knew where he lived. I had one male friend in college who was also a part of my church fellowship, before I met the man who became my husband. I was shy and very awkward around males, but I felt comfortable with those three. Now I know that it was because the light of the God I had come to know as Father was on them. They were good guys, and I could discern that and trusted them.

I remember being exposed to pornography as a teenager. At the house of teenage cousins, my younger brother and I sat as a cousin pulled out a box of VHS tapes of pornography, and we watched and laughed. That experience wasn't good for me. That was a bait of the Satan to put something unclean before my eyes. I was already struggling, and that was just food for the monster. With that, my eye gate was contaminated.

I read somewhere that females are not as visual as males. That may be so, but I am creative and very visual. Watching those videos was spiritually harmful. And I felt condemnation and guilt after watching, yet I wanted to watch more. But God's grace covered me.

I grew up in a very strong fundamentalist Christian church and home. I was taught the word of God and how to apply it in daily living. I memorized Scripture. I participated in and often won Bible Bowl trivia competitions. I knew the Word. The fear I had of God was becoming a deep love, but I was always looking at and focusing on what was wrong with me. I wanted to be perfect for God. I would become depressed as I considered how far from perfection I was, and every time I did something wrong, I would sink into depression with confessions and tears.

One night, I had a dream. In the dream, I was standing in my mother's kitchen. An angel appeared, leaned against the counter, and talked with me. Finally I asked him, "When will I ever be free from these strangleholds on my life?"

He answered, "You will not be free until the day of true repentance."

I woke up and thought about that for many days afterward. True repentance? I was repenting! Every time I did something wrong, I asked forgiveness. Every time I heard a train pass at night, thinking it might be the last trumpet, I would confess my sin and ask forgiveness. I didn't understand until much later that confession, while important, is not true repentance, and neither is asking forgiveness. True repentance is a turning away from a thing that is revealed to be against God's order, not on one's own, but with total dependence on God.

To do that, we must know who we are—our identity in Christ—and that God loves completely and unconditionally. We must know that as His sons and daughters, we can conquer anything. I hadn't fully grasped the significance of that, but I soon would.

After graduation from college, I struggled to find a job. My desire didn't match the plan of God for my life, and I found myself in a self-inflicted struggle. I wanted a job that would give me prestige and money. I knew I was called to preach. I had accepted that fact by age sixteen, and the areas of notable gifting suggested that I needed to teach. I ran from that. There was not much prestige in that, and certainly not any money.

Although I grew up with college-educated parents, we were economically disadvantaged and struggled financially during the 70s and 80s. I knew how to struggle and still succeed. But I didn't want to have to struggle anymore. I ran. I ran as fast and as far away from my call and gift as I could. But everywhere I ran, I ran into closed doors.

I worked in the political realm. I hated it. I worked various other jobs that I hated and that made me feel as invisible and ineffective as I had felt as a child and teen. I didn't realize that I was trying to be something I was not wired to be or it was not time for me to walk into. As it was once written, "If you ask a fish to climb a tree, he will be made to feel stupid."

Finally, after being jobless for seven months and having too much pride to go back home, and after applying at restaurants and bookstores and not being hired, even with my degree from Texas A&M University that I thought would certainly open up employment opportunities with its great network of former students, I accepted that for that season in my life, I was to teach. God wanted to teach me some things as I was teaching that were going to be vital later in ministry. The student was ready, and so the teacher came.

As a teacher and as a spiritual student, I learned. And it turned out that I loved teaching. I felt in alignment. I felt free. I was at peace with my calling and with my work. But silently, I was still struggling with demons from my childhood.

One day, as I was on my lunch break, sitting in my car and struggling with thoughts that were sinful for me, I heard the voice of the Lord audibly for the first time say, "I have sanctified you for myself." The voice was like the sound of waves hitting the shore everywhere around me like surround sound. That was all He said, but it was enough.

Those words changed my life. Even now, in times when I want to quit because the battle is so intense and nothing seems to be going right, I remember those words. All my life, I had struggled to please Him and felt like a failure. But in the place of struggle, He spoke to me, and said that I was His. He loved me unconditionally and completely, and there was nothing I could do about it. Nothing I could do would make him love me less or more. His love was perfect.

I smiled as tears rushed down to my lap. I was going to need that knowledge for the battles ahead. There have been many times that I have gone to preach and have not wanted to go. There have been times when I've asked the Lord to allow me to do something else. But in the end, I kept going, and as I went, joy returned. I kept going because I had experienced His great love. I would do my work for Him despite how I felt at the moment. I would do what I did with all my heart to honor him even if I couldn't see my way. I would not give the adversary the satisfaction of stopping. I would not give up.

Steadfast and Immovable

If you are in a position of leadership, and you feel hopeless and often wonder what it is all for, whatever you do, don't forget Christ's love. Recall to mind often why you started. Do not allow yourself to faint or give up. If you do not stop, you will reap.

Be steadfast and immovable, always abounding in the work of the Lord. Your labor is not in vain. Gross darkness covers the earth, but His light has come, and His glory has risen upon us.

You pray for the sick; you visit the bereaved; you spend time with the Lord beyond your personal devotion to hear His word for His people. You fast; you pray. You look for ways to mature your congregation, to help them relentlessly pursue God, to know who they are in Him, to know the hope of His calling. You deal with the wounds of spirit, soul, and body. You preach to five as you would to five thousand and to five thousand as you would to five.

Your character matches your words. You lead by example. If you ask others not to use foul language, you don't use it. You tell others not to commit adultery, and you submit yourself to God so that you don't commit adultery. You encourage many. You are faithful. You know His word and believe His promises.

Yet there are times when you become weary. At times, you may feel ineffective, depressed, and alone. You want to cry out for help. You entertain thoughts of early retirement or dream about a time when you can go to the back of a church service and just enjoy.

Elijah the prophet found himself in the same place (as did many other leaders of God's people). Immediately after a major victory over the prophets of Baal, in which the confused, vacillating people of God were brought to the point of decision—if God be God, serve Him, and if Baal be God, serve him—he found himself depressed, lamenting over the hardness of the hearts of the people. He withdrew. He felt he had no one to talk to. No one would understand. No one would help.

At times, everything in you may want to cry out, "Help!" But you remember that although many will say they want transparency in their leaders, the truth of the matter is they could not handle the complexity of the depth of your inner struggle, the exhilaration of the highs of winning souls and encouraging others, and the depths of feeling ineffective, judged, inadequate, and burdened. You remember that those around you look to you for leadership and the answer from God as to how to get out of the pits of despair.

You ask yourself, "How can I lead the blind, being blinded at the moment myself?" You can't be human. You can't show emotion. So you withdraw. You put on your face and you faithfully execute your duty as a minister. You never let anyone know the great pain you're experiencing. You minister to those in pain from a place of pain and inner turmoil. This is not the place where God wants you to remain.

As leaders, we must ask the Lord to lead us to and connect us to those with whom we can share our struggles and matters of the heart. But even when He leads us to those people, we must be careful not to put them in the place of the Holy Spirit, our comforter, our guide, and our affirmer. We have to take all of our concerns to Jesus first, receive the rest from Him, and then allow Him to minister to us through those He has chosen.

God is in control. He is God, and we are not. We can't change people. But God changes the stony hearts of men. We can't change the spots of the leopard, but He can. We can't make the vision come to pass, but the Lord will make the vision come to pass, in His own time. We submit to Him and choose to enjoy the journey by focusing on those things that are lovely and true—the victory and not the defeat, the ones who "got it" and not the ones who refused to change. We focus on what He has called us to do and that only, not the results.

One sows, another waters, but God causes the increase. The burden becomes lighter when we allow ourselves to know that He is actually carrying us as we carry the burden. We are not responsible for the results or the fruit to the point that we have made ourselves responsible. We are responsible only to be a vessel of obedience and honor through the empowerment of His Holy Spirit.

Pastors and leaders, stop it! Stop competing with one another, pointing the finger at one another in criticism, and comparing yourselves to others. Instead, encourage one another. Pray for one another. Affirm one another. Send each other messages of encouragement. Text and call one another. Love one another. We need each other.

Be refreshed as you exhort one another and experience the resurrection power of Jesus that will quicken your mortal bodies and satisfy your soul.

So if there is any encouragement in
Christ, any incentive of love, any
participation in the Spirit, any affection
and sympathy, complete my joy by being
of the same mind, having the same love,
being in full accord and of one mind.
—Philippians 2:1-2 (RSV)

CHAPTER 5

Pioneer

She used to sit under the palm tree of
Deborah between Ramah and Bethel
in the hill country of Ephraim, and the
Bnei-Yisrael came to her for judgement.
—JUDGES 4:5

I often thought about Deborah. The more I studied her, the more I identified with her. I loved nature and sitting outside or taking long walks, talking to God. I loved looking up at the sky searching for figures in the clouds. I loved gazing up at the stars in the night sky. Being outdoors in solitude was a place of serenity and refreshing.

Deborah sat under a palm tree. It seemed to be a place of refuge for her as well as a place of work. It was interesting to me that as she would sit, people would come to her. She didn't have to go and recruit people; they came to her, in her seated place—in her place of solitude, where she was refreshed. I'm sure she was drained, as she counseled them from sunup to sundown, but she was seated in her sphere of influence, in the place she was created to function. The place bore her name, even though it was named for one who lived before her time. It was as if the place waited for her to come and sit.

I noticed that people would come to me as if I had stamped on my head, "Come, tell me your hurts and lay your burdens on me, for I care for you." I am an introvert and am drained by too much social interaction. And I felt inadequate, as though I really had nothing to offer other than a smile and a great listening skills. So I smiled and listened. I later learned that was enough. I was enough. But God was more than enough.

I began to understand through my interactions with those who came to me that I could give them God! I would give His words and not my own. That understanding took so much pressure off me. I could be refreshed under the tree, and they could come and receive what had been given to me as I was refreshed.

As a leader, Father will bring you to the place of realization that you are enough. He has supplied you with all of the faith you need to complete the assignment He has given you. He has given you the grace you need and the gifts you need. And He will cause you to sit down and rest in His ability to meet the needs of the people He calls you to.

Fathers

As a child, I prayed that God would make me like Moses or one of the patriarchs or prophets. Elijah was my hero. I loved how he was led by God and was provided for by God. The kind of intimacy of relationship he had with God and the great exploits he did for God inspired me.

Elijah was attacked by a spirit that we call Jezebel, a spirit that carried the name of the woman it famously worked through to torment Elijah and bring spiritual apathy and complacency to the people of God. The effects of her attacks on the people caused Elijah to go into a state of depression and heaviness. He went into the wilderness, away from it all, and there had an encounter with the refreshing presence of God. In a cave, he experienced the wind of God and received a word that put him back on mission.

Like my hero, I experienced the heaviness of nonattainment, the feeling that my work was in vain, that what I was doing was of no effect. I started seeking affirming word and validation, but unlike Elijah, who went to be alone, I searched out spiritual fathers. On Christian television and in the atmosphere during that time, the word on everyone's lips, the common language, seemed to be about "mantles" and how all believers needed someone to mantle and father them in the natural realm. I went out seeking a spiritual father.

I had a wonderful spiritual mother from my home church, a powerful prayer warrior and kind prophet who encouraged me in some of my darkest times. She continues to be that for me. Her husband, the pastor of the church in which I grew up, was a kind man. He took interest in the youth of the congregation, and I learned a lot from him and always felt safe with him. But when I was older and living in a different city, I was disconnected from him, and I did not have a spiritual man other than my husband who took interest in me to pour into me and affirm me.

My natural father was present while I was growing up, but although he was affectionate, I never felt truly connected to him. He was young when I was born. He was a college student, a world-class athlete and world-record holder. He was popular with a bright future. Then I came along. I have often wondered if part of the disconnect I felt was discerned spiritually. Perhaps it was that emphatic part of me that picked up on his feelings, even in my childhood. Maybe it was a feeling that he missed an opportunity or had something taken when I came into his life that caused me to not feel wanted.

He certainly tried to be a good father. I remember the goodnight hugs and kisses and nightly family prayers he led. I remember him tickling me and my brother and playing kickball in the backyard with us. I remember Monopoly and how he was always the banker. I remember him teaching me how to drive my first standard and how he laughed through clenched teeth as I burned the clutch—or pretended to have a heart attack when I grazed mailboxes in our neighborhood. I remember how proud he looked at my college graduation and how he kissed me as he raised my veil on my wedding day. He tried his best. Yet I never really felt accepted. And the memories of how he wasn't there for me, how he hurt my mother, and the words spoken in anger would cloud the good times and words spoken in tenderness.

As a child, I remember hearing one of his close relatives say, "I don't think she's his. She's too bright." *Bright* was a reference to the tone of my skin. After hearing that, I wondered if he felt the same. Whether the rejection was real or just my perception, it hung over me like a heavy cloud. I wanted him to be proud of me and worked hard for his acceptance, but I never felt he saw value in me. As a young girl, when we played football in the backyard, I always wanted to be Earl Campbell, because my dad liked him, and I loved the sound in his voice when he talked about how I "ran all over those boys, just like Earl."

The nonacceptance I felt left a void in my life that drew me closer to Father God, but it also caused me later to seek spiritual fathers, men to be proud of me and affirm me. Later, as my dad was in the last days of his fight with stage 4 lung cancer, he said to me, "Ty, you wrote in a post once that you just wanted me to be proud of you. I am proud of you. I always have been."

His wife went to the head of his bed and took out a picture of him holding me in his arms playfully when I was in my early twenties and gave it to me. She said, "Your dad insisted that this be at the head of his bed." I could no longer hold back the tears that I had been blocking with a polite smile.

When I walked into his house, I looked around and saw pictures of his oldest daughter and her children, but none of me, my children, or my brothers. My heart was aching. The familiar feelings of rejection were fighting to regain control. But Father God had me there that day not just for me to see my dad again but so that I could be healed. I didn't want to be there, but I went because I wanted to honor my Father God by honoring my dad. In doing so, I was healed, and a void was filled.

Before my father-wound was healed, I was in search of someone to mantle me. In prayer one day, I felt the Spirit of God impress upon my spirit this question and statement: "Who mantled Elijah? Elijah surely mantled Elisha, but no one knew where Elijah came from or who his mother or father was. There are always firsts … pioneers … to begin a new thing." After that, I stopped asking. I heard in Father's reply that He himself would mantle me and that in due season, He would use me to mantle others.

When I reached a place of peace where I could lay aside the issue of spiritual fathers and mantles that were brought on by words that well-intentioned leaders released into the atmosphere but did not, I learned, apply to me and many others with a calling similar to mine, I was able to move on. And God sent a man to stand in the place of a spiritual father to me. I trusted him, although because of things I had seen in ministry, I did not trust many. He had been an influence in my life when I was a teen as my Sunday school teacher and youth leader, but he had moved away before I graduated high school. Although he lived in a different state—he was in Louisiana and I was in Texas—he prayed for me often and sent words of encouragement and aid to me and my husband and our ministry fellowship. He invested in me and demonstrated confidence in me, inviting me to be a guest minister at his church.

The Lord has sent others also to speak into my life and propel me forward. When we wait upon the Lord, we do well. He makes everything beautiful in its time. He was causing the pain of nonacceptance to diminish.

Women in Ministry

A female who pastors in a rural area will experience, in most cases, nonacceptance. I was no exception. Being a female who was also black and young made the adventure even more challenging ... and delightful. When I went to various ministry-related events with my husband, most people would not even engage me in conversation but would ask questions of my husband even after he repeatedly tried to redirect them to me. I didn't get offended. My pastor in ministry had told me and demonstrated before me the truth that one should never defend a call to ministry or try to prove anything. Never strive or fight for a platform. Just be.

I understood that there were many blacks who would go and sit under non-black leadership, but there were not many whites who would sit under black leadership, let alone black female leadership. That is a problem of history and culture that has not been healed. And our lack of desire to change or inability to see the need for change gave place to principalities of division, racism, and ideology, and they had a stronghold, even in churches. That battle could only be won in prayer as we turned our hearts to God as a people, as a nation.

I understood that my part was to not actively engage in spiritual warfare against those principalities by binding and loosing and declaring and decreeing, but to war in a different way by teaching the people through word and deed a different way of thinking and seeing and loving—the Jesus way, the way of the Word. We gave them place and power, and we could take place and power back as we walked out and spoke out the Word.

As I was working with multiple generations and multiple ethnicities, I often fought off feelings of rejection, disrespect, and condescension. One older gentleman said to me once, "You're too good-looking to be a pastor." He was kind, but there was a thought behind the comment regarding standards of beauty, women's work, and acceptance that I didn't like. I'm glad Father God does not look at outward appearance, but rather judges the heart.

My heart was for God. I wanted to be seen as His servant and as holy. I didn't want people to see my gender in a way that would hinder them from hearing His word. I was comfortable in my femininity and in the unique way ministry was demonstrated through me as a woman. I wouldn't feel compelled to try to fit into the suit of a man or take on the sound of a man. But neither did I try to take on the sound of a woman. Although I was very comfortable in my black skin and understood the value of my black voice, I didn't want a black sound. I wanted the sound of Heaven—for the voice of God to be released through me and for my life to be an expression of His love and power that brings healing and unity.

As a female pastor, there are sometimes waters I have to navigate that my male counterparts may not have to navigate in the same way. I have learned that even though we shouldn't judge by outward appearance, we do, and I must be careful of my dress. My husband prefers for me to wear robes and ministerial apparel when I deliver the word. Even though that felt at first overly religious and pretentious to me, I complied because the ministerial garb points to His holiness and covers gender and sexuality, and most of all because I love, honor, and submit to my husband. There are times when I do not wear robes, but whether in a robe or in trendy clothing, I ask myself, "Does this represent the Kingdom well? Does it honor my Father?"

When I wear a robe, I feel the weight of the position I stand in and the responsibility of the privilege to stand as a priest of my God, representing His holiness, but even the robes do not solve all the problems associated with the eye. The eyes are windows to the soul. And if the soul has lust and perversion, whatever the eye sees will be perverted to reflect that.

Once as I was ministering to a young man at the altar, I discerned his thoughts. I was bending down to lay hands on his knee for healing, and I heard vulgar thoughts. And although I was experienced in word of knowledge and discerning of spirits, especially as I did altar ministry and in prayer, I was new to this operation and dimension of the prophetic in which I heard clearly what another was thinking. I believe that everything God does and allows, He does and allows with purpose. He doesn't reveal to embarrass or just to give knowledge. Knowledge is to be appropriated. When I heard those thoughts, I knew there was another spirit present and a greater need than the healing of the knee. I didn't have to stop ministering because of the perverted thoughts. The thoughts had less to do with my femininity as than with his greater need. So I ministered healing to his soul first.

Manifestation of Healing

When we first began ministry, God spoke that we were a healing ministry. We laid hands on people expecting them to be healed. Many were healed, but many more were not. We saw babies born deaf hear again, and we saw visible tumors disappear. Many were healed of nagging sicknesses, and others were delivered from demons. But there were many others in whom we did not see sudden manifestations of healing and deliverance. I did not get discouraged; we just kept praying and believing.

I did, however, want answers as to why some were healed and some were not so that we could be more effective. When I looked at the life of Jesus, I saw that all who were oppressed of the devil were healed by Jesus when he came into contact with them. What was wrong with us? I understood that God didn't change. His Word was the same. He healed then, and he heals now. So what was the fly in the oil of the apothecary?

After some very notable bold declarations with no manifestation, God sent us a word of encouragement to cause us to keep pressing and to keep our expectations high and our focus on Him. Father God sent a word to us through one of His servants that confirmed what we felt, what we had heard, and what we expected, having read and believed His Word. We were a healing ministry. People in ambulances would tell the drivers, "Get me to BOLD!" The word seemed to tarry, but we had learned that ours was not to figure out dates and times, nor was ours the responsibility of results. Ours was but to be obedient and go! As the olive is pressed to produce oil, the healing ministry came and is increasing with the press.

As a child, I suffered with asthma. I was often in and out of hospitals, and there were many times, my mother told me, when she thought I was going to die. But when I was nine, my mother took me to our church camp meeting. An evangelist, VV Lister, who worked in the ministry of divine healing, was present and laying hands on the sick. He laid hands on me that day and prayed. After that day, I never had an attack of asthma.

Later, I understood that the spirit of rejection often gives entry to breathing disorders like asthma, and that rejection had anchored asthma in my wounded soul, but it was cast out also on that day when I was healed. What Jesus does, He does well. And whom the Son sets free, is free indeed! There were so many things my Father God set me free from. And there were other things I knew that although I had not experienced the manifestation of healing yet, it was mine and it would come. He had done it before. I knew He would do it again.

As an infant, I suffered with anemia and had many struggles with iron deficiency throughout my adult life. In my early thirties, I was diagnosed with a brain tumor. I knew God as healer, but for six months, my mind was a battlefield. I would fight thoughts of, *You won't live to see your daughters married. Your son is so young, he won't even remember you. You're going to die.* I had to remember the words that had been spoken over me that I had written in my journals—the ones that had not come to pass yet and brought me distress because of it. Now I was glad they had not come to pass, because I knew that God is not capable of lying. He said it. It had not come to pass yet. So I couldn't die!

I reminded myself of that fact whenever a negative thought came to mind. I would live and not die. After a time of intense prayer and fasting with my home church, I went back after six months for another MRI. The report from my neurosurgeon agreed with what we believed as we prayed: the tumor was gone. I was healed.

Every time I have an opportunity, I will pray for the sick and all who are oppressed. I know God as healer. His timing is impeccable and His plans are perfect, even when we cannot understand the timing or the plan.

CHAPTER 6

Lapidoth:
The Men in the Life of the Warrior Woman

Now Deborah, a prophet, the wife of
Lapidoth, was leading Israel at that time.
—*Judges 4:4*

Most women will have three significant male relationships: the Father, the Partner, and the Son. It is a relationship standard we also find for the Church, as she also has three significant relationships: Father, Holy Spirit, and Son. God loves to reveal Himself in threes. There are three parts to our self: spirit, soul, and body. There are three parts to a song: melody, rhythm, and harmony. Jesus often sent His disciples out in threes. A threefold cord is not easily broken, and things are established, according to Scripture, by the testimony of two or three witnesses.

Deborah had three significant male relationships: with the commander of the army of Israel, Barak, as a partner in war; with the men and warriors of Israel as sons who came to her for her counsel and judgments; and with Lapidoth, her husband, who was a type of the Father or covering for her.

The name *Lapidoth* gives us some indication of the significance of Deborah's husband. He was not just someone in the shadows who waited for Deborah to come home. He had a call that was different from her call yet just as significant. His name means "torch" or "torch-bearer." Rabbinical tradition holds that he was one who trimmed the wicks of the candles in the temple. He kept a place with no windows or natural means of light lit by trimming the wick—cutting away what needed to be cut away—and He was also the one who trimmed Deborah's wick to keep her burning brightly as a torch for Israel.

My husband is my Lapidoth. He trims my wick. If you burn candles often, you know how important it is to trim the wicks. The only time you do not trim a wick is at the first lighting. Trimming the wick helps with burn quality and the appearance of the flame. Untrimmed wicks cause unnecessary smoke and soot. According to the American Candle Association, candles that are not maintained can be dangerous. That which would provide a pleasant aroma and warm light can cause harm.

The one who trims the wick has to know how the candle burns to know whether to keep the wick trimmed short or longer. My husband watches me and knows me. He knows my facial expressions and what they indicate. He knows how to motivate me and inspire me. He knows when to keep his instruction short and when to go longer in his counsel. He recognizes when my fire is low and I'm just going through the motions. He trims my wick, and he does this well, because God instructs Him. He is a man of God.

He also does this because we cultivated a friendship before marriage. We developed spiritual and emotional intimacy, then sexual intimacy. He is my best friend. I like spending time with him. Just talking with him and laughing with him gives me relief at the end of the hardest day of trial and most intense ministry.

He is very secure in his calling to the mountain of government. Although he works with me in ministry, he has never competed with me. We help each other take the mountains we have been promised, and we go in together. We handle enemies together.

I sense that Father is forming many threefold-cord alliances in this season of husband-and-wife teams with their children and also connecting two or three ministry streams for greater effectiveness. It's no fun winning alone. It's always better together.

We married in 1997, and my husband, Ronnie, has been my best friend and strongest supporter in ministry. He affirms me and encourages me to push beyond my limits. He makes me feel as though I can accomplish anything and reminds me that I can through Christ.

I met Ronnie when we were students at Texas A&M University in College Station, Texas. He followed me to a bookstore on campus and asked me to buy him a folder. I was amused. His humor attracted me to him. But my parents were very protective. Although I was an adult and in college, I still had a curfew, and I wasn't allowed to date. He asked me for my phone number after I purchased the folder for him. I wrote a number on his folder, but it wasn't the right number.

I thought that would be the last time I talked to him, but he was persistent. Somehow—I still don't know how—he got my phone number and called me. This was before cell phones; we only had one phone, and it was in my parents' bedroom. So it was my dad who answered. He called me to the phone and had a look on his face that said, *Make it short and keep it business.*

I was nervous. But the conversation, short as it was, intrigued me, because Ronnie was a good listener. He talked a lot and drew me in, but he also listened. I had never felt listened to before. I never felt that anyone really valued what I had to say. Perhaps that was a consequence of the generation and culture in which I was raised—one in which children were to be seen and not heard. I'm not sure. I have a brother only fifteen months younger than I who seemed to have no problem being seen and heard. So maybe it was just an issue of temperament.

Ronnie listened himself into a relationship. We dated throughout college, and our friendship grew. We had common interests. He loved sports, and although my love wasn't intense like his, we played sports together. We played on an intramural volleyball team. It's important for couples to have things to do together that they enjoy, things that make them laugh, things that help them to grow and mature together.

After seven years of dating, we were married. The first three years were like a dream, and our only challenge was where we would worship. Our spiritual lives were important to both of us, and he knew from the outset of our relationship that I had accepted a call to ministry. He wanted me to be developed in ministry. I wanted us to worship at the same House to be developed together in the Word. But he was raised in a Primitive Baptist church. His church did not accept women in any kind of ministry. We both knew that I would not be developed in ministry there.

I loved the people at Ronnie's church. They were supportive, and in that, they reminded me of the church in which I grew up. Ronnie was emotionally indebted to them because they had been active and supportive in his life since childhood. And since we were living in his hometown, it was difficult for him to leave. I was attending a church in Austin, Texas—Banah Full Community Church. It was a small diverse gathering of Kingdom-minded, very gifted people. It was my training church. The leaders were forerunners, and they built a House of apostolic and prophetic ones who were themselves called to train, equip, and raise up ministers. I was home. But I knew Ronnie was not called there.

He visited with me at times, and I attended his House of Worship at times. Those within his congregation, not knowing that I was a minister, asked me to speak at their women's conferences from time to time. Once they found out I was a minister, however, the invitations decreased. Yet they remained a loving group of people.

After five years of church swapping, I completed my ministry training and was ordained a pastor. My church leadership then launched me out to plant the ministry. They confirmed that I was called to build in Bastrop. I learned a lot that prepared me for this new work at my home church in which I grew up in Bryan, Texas. I had learned much that equipped me for the warfare of apostolic ministry in the fellowship in Austin.

Dr. Valerie Bridgeman and Don Davis gave me a picture of the husband–wife ministry team and how those streams were to flow together for effective ministry. My home church affirmed me and showed me unconditional love, spoke greatness into me, and developed me in the Word with a strong doctrinal foundation. My training church taught me how to wield the staff of leadership that was in my hand. But Ronnie trimmed my wick. He kept the fire pure and burning.

CHAPTER 7

A Mother in Israel

Villages were deserted in Israel,
deserted, until I, Deborah, arose,
a mother in Israel arose.
—Judges 5:7

Deborah is said to have been a prophet and judge in Israel. The nature of her ministry to Israel was also apostolic, even before the time of the apostles. She was a mother in Israel. And although she more than likely had biological children with her husband, Lapidoth, she was undoubtedly a mother in Israel in the way that a man is a father to spiritual sons and daughters.

It is not an easy task to mother, and it is even more challenging to mother many. It requires patience and understanding. It requires vision—the ability to see potential lying underneath, to see and love past the current state to the place of destiny and to help others emerge and go forward. It is work that is often emotionally draining and sometimes thankless.

Sons and daughters come and they go. Some will stay and help you raise children in your home, but most will go to build their own homes. It's sometimes hard to let go of ones you pour into and labor over and love deeply. But Father has taught me to love those deeply that He sends to me, love them to health, but then hold them loosely, because they are His and only lent to me to train or affirm or ordain.

If you are called to leadership in ministry, expect and anticipate the various seasons of relationships. There is the gestation period, where you carry them and a tender affection develops. There is the early childhood stage, where you are growing in love for them while you are training them. You will have to do most of the work, and they will walk behind you as you lead. There is the adolescence stage, where they start to come into their own. They begin to understand their gifts and callings and to function in them.

The adolescent stage is often when Hagars develop. Hagar started to despise her mistress, Sarah, because she learned from Sarah what was important and mastered it. After producing what Sarah had prepared and helped her to produce, she no longer honored Sarah or held her in esteem, because she felt that she could do things Sarah could not. When you go through this stage, do not cast these individuals out as Sarah did Hagar, as tempting as the thought may be. They are not ready to go out, even if they feel they are.

Some will start to question what you do, thinking they can do it better; some may even try to usurp your authority. When this happens, recall the tender moments of gestation and early childhood. Be patient as you navigate this stage and never yield to the temptation to defend yourself or your authority.

I have sent some out who were adolescents but felt they were fully grown, knowing they were not ready, only because I knew that their hearts were no longer with me. They were in the House but not really present. But thank God for His faithfulness. As with Hagar, He took care of them.

At this same adolescent stage is also when you see the spirit of Absalom rise in some. Absalom sat at the gate of the city, the place of entry, and talked to the people about how much better things would be with him as a leader over his father, David. He did this because he felt rejected by his father. Often, when spiritual children feel rejected, abandoned, or overlooked, they will be open to the spiritual influence of this insidious spirit.

Absalom cast doubt with his word as to the effectiveness of his father's leadership and love for the people—all of this because David didn't handle a situation that was important to Absalom in the way he thought it should have been handled. He never expressed his feelings of anger, resentment, and rejection to his father. He let the anger rest in his bosom, and it took root. Soon there was a plot. Although he surely loved his father, his anger and feelings of rejection blinded him and caused him to work against the one who had raised and positioned him.

Absalom started trying to take by manipulation and force what his father was planning to give him as an inheritance as his handsome, beloved son. Absalom wouldn't stop or repent, and the breach was never restored. There was a death in the relationship, and the father was the one who was hurt most. David saw what his son was doing but never confronted him. Perhaps he was too hurt by it to confront it, or perhaps he hoped it would just blow over. But he should have confronted his son. Fathers and mothers must confront what they see, especially in this stage of development in the life of a son or daughter, or a death in the relationship will occur.

Learning to Let Go

I had a daughter in ministry who I loved deeply. I saw so much greatness in her. Her temperament was similar to mine, and connecting with her was just easy. I didn't have to try to be anything for her; I could just be. She would come to my house often, and we would just sit, and that was okay. I was with her as she grew into adulthood, through surgeries and loss and graduations and marriage and birth, through ups and downs. And she was always present for me.

But somehow, I failed to live up to her expectations. That had always been a fear—that getting to know me, I would be a disappointment. I would not be adequate. She separated herself from me for a long while, and I would hear about major occurrences in her life, but not from her. I asked her to come help me in ministry, but she refused. She lost someone close to her, and hearing about it, I came, but I felt an emotional distance, even through her natural graciousness.

After a while, she started writing to me, but what she wrote was very hurtful to me. I stopped reading what she wrote and just had my husband give me a summary, because I needed to guard my heart. The relationship had become toxic, and I had missed it early on, at a time when the breach could have been repaired. She felt that I was not there for her when she needed it most and that I had exposed her to some spiritual things too early that caused her harm. All I could do was reply that I loved her, apologize for missing it with her, and release her. I prayed for her and prayed that Jesus, the Repairer of the Breach, would repair the breaches in our relationship. And I let her go. I loved her still, but I let her go.

I have had other sons and daughter leave. Some have left well, and I launched them out in peace and joy. Others left prematurely in rejection or rebellion. But I trust Father to heal any wounds and guard them from the church hurt that causes many to miss the mark of their high calling or to experience ineffectiveness in ministry and future relationships.

Fathers and mothers have to learn how to nurture and train. They have to learn how to prune and confront. And they have to learn how to let go. Sometimes letting go is easy and celebratory, as we launch sons and daughters into their destiny. At other times, it can be emotionally painful. Either way, we must let go at the time to let go. Having done our best, we trust God to do the rest.

The Challenge of Balance

When I first planted the ministry in Bastrop, I was the mother of a beautiful six-month-old baby girl, Micaela. This was a very challenging time, and again, I was tested with feelings of inadequacy. I was often overwhelmed and had a lack of people resources to support my work. I was used to being able to spend long hours in prayer and study of the Word, but now as a mother, I had to balance the work of ministry and the work of parenting.

One day, as I was crying because I didn't have time to study, I felt the familiar impression of Holy Spirit speak to my spirit: *My grace is sufficient for you. You are prepared for this work. The Word is in you.* This brought me great relief. But there were still things I had to balance that presented a challenge for me.

Sundays were the worst. Before worship, I would have to express milk and prepare diaper bags instead of last-minute sermon prep. Once at worship, I would lead the worship, changing out transparencies with lyrics while my husband pushed the on button of our little boom box. As the songs played, I would run to the restroom to feed my daughter and then come back to preach the sermon. After worship, people would want to talk to me. Some would want on-the-spot counseling because I seemed to have had stamped on my head, *Tell me all your problems and release all your burdens, for I care for you.* I learned later that this was an anointing that drew people and not some invisible sign.

My daughter would cry for my time, but those who were seeking me overlooked her cries. There were times when I had parent guilt because I felt I neglected her, as I was out on 2 a.m. ministry calls with my husband or being pulled away on Sundays or receiving multiple emails or phone calls. But God was gracious, and He sent my mother to minister to us during the early years. She was a tremendous help. I didn't trust anyone to leave my daughter with; I had heard too many stories of early childhood abuse from those I counseled. So had my mother not been there, I would have still done ministry, but with a baby in tow it would not have been as effective.

Once, after feeding my daughter in the restroom during worship, I came out to preach and looked for my sermon notes. These were the days before I realized I was a Navi, when I preached homiletically sound sermons with three points, where I told them what I was going to tell them and then told them. I needed those notes. That was a well-constructed sermon.

I sent my husband back home to get the sermon notes, and I stalled with more worship songs and testimonies. He returned with no notes. I was furious. But I remembered the words the Holy Spirit had spoken to me earlier: *My grace is sufficient for you. You have been prepared for this work. And my word is in you.* I got up to preach for the first time without any notes. The word flowed as I yielded to the Holy Spirit. And as I did, I heard myself saying things I had not prepared to say, and thought to myself, *Ooh, that's good. I want to go back and listen to that.*

I found out later that I was a Navi, a prophetic vessel from whom the Word bubbles up and over spontaneously. That moment propelled me into the place in which I was created to stand: the place I was formed for in my mother's womb, the place that been confirmed when I was eighteen.

First Ministry Among Many

I have two other children. I was blessed to be able to license them both as ministers of the gospel, and it gives me such delight to hear them preach and watch them work in ministry. I was given three beautiful blessings from the Lord. And over the years, Father God has been teaching me how to balance all things and to keep first things first. My children are a "first thing," and home is my first ministry among many ministries.

I had seen many pastor's kids turn from ministry with disdain. I didn't want this for my children, and my husband and I vowed to hold each other accountable that we would not get so busy saving the world that we lost our own children. Father has shown me that I can't be everything for people. No matter how I try, I will always fall short. He reminds me to keep first things first and allow Him to take care of the things that are His alone to take care of. He reminds me in those times when I start to feel overwhelmed with parent guilt that He is my source and He is the answer. He is God, and I am not.

He whispers to me again and again, "My grace is sufficient for you. You are an arrow in my hand, and my oil is upon the arrow. You will accomplish what I send you out to accomplish." In times when I felt insufficient to deal with the problems of the parishioners in my care, He reminded me that He would not share His glory with another. He would not allow me to become an idol in anyone's life and wanted me to teach them how to see Him, how to hear Him, and how look to Him for themselves. He was the Desire of Nations, and He died for the people—I didn't have to. All I had to do was give my life obediently to Him and rest in Him. All I had to do was sit under the tree, as Deborah had done, in my place of authority.

He freed me from captivity to a messiah complex and a martyr spirit. He freed me to be. He has freed you to be the unique one He created you to be! Just be.

There were times when my children would cry for my attention and those seeking ministry would not be moved by their cries, but hungry for God through me, would push in all the more. As a young mother and pastor, I had to learn to say no to people and set boundaries. I had read the book *Boundaries* by Drs. Townsend and Cloud, but in my desire to be everything for everyone, I ignored the good advice and warnings contained in the book and was losing my soul. I was drained. I felt guilty when I wasn't at the hospital for this one, at the nursing home for that one, or at this event with that one. I felt guilty taking time with my family and even more so for myself.

I felt terrible and was sick often. I looked terrible—older than my age. How could I enjoy a vacation and post smiling pictures when so many were hurting? My mother often told me to take some time away. She advised wisely that I couldn't be my best for God or the people if I was worn out. "Even Jesus went to the mountain or pushed off in a boat to escape and recharge," she would say. But I value heroics and exploits. I somehow felt it heroic to push myself mercilessly. It seemed brave to preach until I felt I would pass out because I was fighting through fatigue and illness.

But Father was speaking to me of the foolishness of this. And finally, I began to listen. As my children got older, those words my mother and other wise ones spoke to encourage me to rest began to resonate more. I didn't want to miss the important events in my children's lives because I worked myself to death. And I reflected that over the years, the ones I had given my all to and at time neglected my home for had moved on—some even in offense because I could not be everything for them. The more I gave, the more they required. It seemed that there was always a need unmet.

I began to understand and put all the pieces together from the painful experiences of the past to grasp the significance of the truth that I could never fill their emptiness or completely meet their need because it was a God-sized void. There were places only He could fill. It took years to wrap my mind around the significance of self-care and the importance of family as a first ministry. But when I got it, I got it, and I became a happier me.

Remember to keep first things first. Seek first the Kingdom of God and His righteousness. Seek the Helper, not the help; the one who promised, not the promise. Father God has promised that if we do, all the things we were longing for would be added to us, and the things we would have chased after would chase us. When you rest in this revelation, you will be a happier you.

CHAPTER 8

Deborah's Song

Then Deborah and Barak son of Abinoam sang on that day saying; 'When the leaders take the lead in Israel, when the people freely offer themselves.
—JUDGES 5:1–2

Everything I had experienced in my life prepared me for the work to which I was called and for which I was formed. Everything you have experienced—every trial, every failure, every victory —has prepared you for what you were created for. You were formed and fashioned in your mother's womb for a purpose. Your personality and temperament were given by divine design so that you might be fully equipped for the work for which you were created.

You were created to win, to live a victorious life, to rule and reign on the earth that Father God created. You were created to advance His Kingdom, to produce, to steward what He gave and multiply it. Father is always processing and preparing us for what is before us.

All the judges of Israel before Deborah won some war that allowed them to enter the office of judge in Israel. We are not told in the Book of Judges what wars Deborah led in and won that opened the door for her to become the leader of her people. When we are introduced to her, she is already accepted as a leader and is leading the people. Perhaps this was strategic on the part of Father God to not include that information in her narrative. It certainly illustrates well the fact that many times, we see leaders in positions of honor and glory, but we don't know their process or story. We see them rise and think the rise was sudden, when there were years of preparation and struggle, faith leaps, and faith purchases before they reached that place of what appears to be a sudden ascent.

Deborah sings a song of victory at the end of the battle she led the people in for freedom from their oppressor. In it, she recognized God as the true hero of the story, as the great deliverer. She knew that it was not by her hand or Barak's might or Jael's cunning that this victory came. God placed her in position and gave her instructions, and she obeyed. She recognized that they could not aid God with military might. It was God who created the perfect storm, the river of mud that caught the chariots of war and disabled them that caused the war to be won. She obeyed God and rose up as an apostolic leader to set order and bring government to the people in a time when "the villages were deserted in Israel."

From her song, it seems that she was chosen by the people to lead because of her wisdom. Nobles came to her to ask her to lead. She led with a mighty man of war, Barak, beside her. But the final blow to the enemy was given by another woman, Jael. She, like Deborah, was a married woman. Her husband was not weak—he was off fighting—but she was chosen and given the honor of defeating the enemy.

Many times, it is assumed that strong women have weak husbands and female leaders either do not have husbands or are not submissive to their husbands. The Bible in the story of Deborah shows that this does not have to be the case. Women can be strong while their husbands, too, are strong. A woman can lead in various arenas, protecting and providing for others while her husband leads, provides for, and protects her and the family in the home. They can lead in one area as their husbands lead in another, and the leadership of the one does not diminish the leadership of the other.

In the Garden, God created man. He created mankind as male and female and gave them dominion and the command to subdue the earth and multiply. The woman and the man were created with complementary parts and gifts to complement one another and allow them to advance together and make the world that God called good even better. With God as a third in the binding cord, they made it the best it could be.

Women can be feminine and lead. They do not have to take on the voice of a man. When they realize their identity in Christ and their uniqueness, they can lead well. They discover their voice, see value in the gifts they've been given, and respect the unique ways those gifts are meant to operate through them as chosen vessels. They lead with strength.

Jael was feminine. She was gracious. She was wise. She offered Sisera, the commander of the enemy army, some milk, recognizing that he was tired and honoring him as a warrior. When he fell asleep, she stabbed him in the head with a tent peg. This was the time of Deborah and of Jael. It was appointed twice for women to rise to bring deliverance and to stand with the men against the oppressor.

This is also an appointed time when God calls His daughters to rise against the adversary, to lead with their brothers and husbands, to lead in the way that He has equipped them to lead, with faith in Him as their great deliverer. The year 2016 was surely the year of the peg (the Hebrew year Ayin Vav), when the House of God was made secure by pruning and exposing and by teaching and equipping. The Word came into demonstration in the lives of the people of God in greater measure.

Because God is ordered in all things and purposeful, the year 2017 was a time that continued and built upon what began the previous year. It was a time when the Jaels began to rise and pull up the peg—the word of God—to put to death the Siseras, the enemies of the movement of God. It was the beginning of the time, the opening of the door for the Deborahs to rise and awaken the warriors out of complacency and religious old-wineskin mindsets into glory realms and train them for Kingdom exploits.

It is God's set time for Kingdom glory. Many things began to shift during those years. It was the start of something new—a time when ancient gates that had been sealed closed were opening. I perceived that women would play a more significant and prominent role in the new thing that was emerging.

At her feet he [Sisera] bowed, he fell, he lay down: at her feet he bowed, there he fell dead.

—JUDGES 5:27

Victory

There was war in Heaven, and Satan was cast out of Heaven to earth (Revelation 12:7–10). Jesus tells us that He saw Satan fall from Heaven like lightning (Luke 10:18). Since the rebellion of Satan and the fallen ones, there has been war in the heavens and war on the earth, and there are no demilitarized zones. You are on one side or the other. There are only ever two choices: life or death, narrow way or broad way, blessing or cursing, light or darkness, God or Baal. But Father has promised that in the end, we win. He calls us more than conquerors in Christ Jesus (Romans 8:37). We win because God cloaked Himself in humanity and came to earth to live as a man.

The prophet Isaiah tells us that God marveled that there was no intercessor to stand in the gap for man, so He did it himself (Isaiah 59:16). Scripture tells us that cursed or anathema is anyone who hangs from a tree (Galatians 3:13); in fulfillment of this prophetic word, Jesus allowed Himself to be hung upon the tree in the form of a cross and not only took the curse upon His body that was meant for us but became the curse for us. He died for us so that we could have life in abundance and the second death which involves Hell would have no power over us. He paid the penalty for our sins. I don't know why He loves us so, but He does, and I am grateful. He died and won our freedom, giving us the opportunity to be reconciled to Father God through His blood sacrifice, for it is written that there is no remission of sins except by the shedding of blood (Hebrews 9:22).

But the narrative didn't end there. When He died, he also rose again. When He rose, there was a local resurrection of the dead, in which graves were opened and the dead walked the streets of Jerusalem, showing themselves to many (Matthew 27:52). That local resurrection foreshadowed the resurrection of the dead at Jesus's second coming. Jesus did not go to Hell to finish atoning for us. That was finished at the cross when He said, "Tetelestai, it is finished!" (John 19:30). He descended so that those who were waiting in Paradise could ascend. He went and preached to those who had died, justified only by the law. And accepting His testimony and Him as their Messiah, they were resurrected, making him the first fruits of those who would be raised to life (1 Corinthians 15:20).

On the third day according to the Jewish accounting of days from evening to evening, Jesus was resurrected from the dead. After showing Himself to many for forty days, He was taken up to heaven and is now seated at the right hand of the Father in power, waiting to return to catch those up who love His appearing in the clouds to be with Him, the dead in Christ being raised first. The Scripture teaches us that when Jesus ascended, He held captivity captive, and He gave gifts to men (Ephesians 4:8). The gifts He gave were given so that the ones who believed in Him could be trained and equipped for good works and to occupy and advance until He returned, bringing others into the Kingdom, being fruitful and multiplying in number, becoming an ever expanding Kingdom. The advancing ones were given the instruction to go and make disciples, to baptize men and teach them, to share the message of life and love with them, and He promised that everyone who called upon the name of the Lord would be saved (Romans 10:13).

Jesus paid the penalty for our sins. He took the punishment for our sins upon Himself. All we have to do is accept His free gift, and we can live a life of fulfillment and victory—a life of love, joy, and peace even in times of struggle and darkness. If we confess with our mouths the Lord Jesus and believe in our hearts that God has raised Him from the dead, we will be saved (Romans 10:9). Do you want to be all you were created to be? Do you want your life to count for something so that your living is not in vain? You can begin today.

Ask Jesus to be your Lord and Savior and to come into your life. Renounce all sinful acts from your past and ask Him to make you clean and to teach you His ways. Confess that you are a sinner and that He is the Son of God. Renounce all sinful acts from your past. And as you do this in faith, you are accepted. Your name is written in His Book of Life, and you will never taste of the second death or see Hell. You are now on the side of light and on a journey of discovery where you will know your God and know who you are in Him.

The angels of Heaven are rejoicing, and Father God is rejoicing over you with singing. You are a new creation in Christ Jesus now. It's time to step into the new.

Going Forward

Every year I seek the Lord for vision and direction for the next year. As a leader, I crave truth and clarity of direction—an Issachar anointing to discern the times and know what to do. I seek a clear picture of where I'm going and what to expect so that I can lead effectively. I understand that if the blind lead the blind, they both fall into a pit. I was careful to walk in a way that would not cause another to fall and sought revelation so that I could stand and help others to stand. Father has been faithful to give revelation and direction as I seek Him.

Early in my ministry, I starting studying the Hebrew language. The alphabet and connected numbers and pictures intrigued me. It is a tripartite language of word, picture, and letter. I saw the connection between the three-in-one God, the three-part heavens, the three parts of music, the three dimensions, and the tripartite man. Deep things are revealed in threes and often confirmed by three witnesses.

I began to see relevance in the plan of God for each year through what was revealed by the Holy Spirit in the Hebrew alphabet. I didn't see it in an esoteric, mystical, crystal-ball kind of way but as a message from a God who is ordered in all things—purposeful and precise about Himself, His Son, His Kingdom, and His people—regarding doorways of possibilities that open each year. The release of revelation for the new year is not to stop what was started in the previous year; it is more of a release of revelation to give permission to go up another step, to enter into another realm. It is a doorway of possibility. We can choose to walk in the revelation of the new year and embrace something new and on purpose while building on what was revealed previously or stay in the place we came to by what was revealed in previous years.

For example, the first letter of the Hebrew alphabet is *Aleph*. Aleph has the numeric value of one, and the picture is that of an ox, the symbol of strength. When Jesus says that he is the Alpha (Greek) or Aleph (Hebrew), He is speaking of more than just being the first. He is also the beast of burden, the ox who carries our burdens, and he is our strong, mighty, valiant one. He is unrivaled.

Yet another example is found in the year 2017, or 5777 on the Hebrew calendar. As I sought revelation about that year, I was revealed to (as were many other leaders around the world) about the sword. The sword is both a ruling sword and a dividing sword. The pictograph for 7 is a crowned man with a sword in hand. It symbolizes victory in war. That year was to be a time of preparation for war—prepared by the teachings and with the realization of who Jesus is and who we are in Him—and a time of separation to rule.

I saw that 2017 was to be a year of distinction. And it was. As in the days of Elijah's showdown at Mount Carmel, Father made a distinction among His people with fire on the water, calling them to the point of decision in terms of who they would serve. It was a year of purging, pruning, cleansing, and winnowing (separation between wheat and tare and the removal of chaff). The people of God began to be separated from things and people who had hindered their progress for a long time. On the world front, it was a time of separation and preparation. Much of what is happening now at the gate of government is in preparation for what is to come. All the shaking and shifting is making way for the new.

September 21, 2017, began the year 5778 with Yom Teruah. It was to be a time of Chet. Chet has the numeric value of 8 and is a picture of a wall, fence, gateway, or doorway. The letter Chet also resembles a ladder. The Chet is the doorway you pass through to get to one place from another. It is not the door. Dalet, the letter with numeric value 4 is the door. 1n 2014, the focus was on Jesus as the door, and the leaders of the people were called to teach about the new man and our position in Christ. Chet is not the door but more of a gateway, signifying crossing over into something new, immediately with no delay, or a hallway of transition.

The season of transition was ending. It was crossover time. The year 5778 was a time to begin crossing over into the promise. But there was a promise of more later. The journey was not finished. We began to occupy, and we advanced and occupied until Jesus returned.

Other aspects of the doorway and the ladder stand out. When Jacob fled from his brother Esau, he had a vision of a ladder coming from heaven upon which angels were ascending and descending, and there was an open heaven or a gateway/doorway above it. He recognized that He met with God there and called the name of the place Beth El, because he said that was the House of God. Interesting to me, too, that

Scripture takes the time to mention that he laid His head on a rock. Nothing in Scripture is random. I see the rock he laid upon as a symbol of Jesus. There was revelation given in that place about redemption. We receive godly revelation that leads to resolution when we have our minds on Jesus—when we seek intimacy of relationship with Him. The time of the vision of the ladder is dated to 1948, a time of Chet!

Jacob had another life-changing encounter before he crossed over from one place to another. He had to wrestle with an angel. This was a time of resolution for him, the time of healing of yet open wounds, where he had to face his fear so that he could recover. It was a time when an enemy was made to be at peace. In order to enter Canaan, Jacob had to pass through Edom, the land of the brother he had wronged. He had to face his brother Esau and come face to face with his past—his past sin and past failure and disappointments—so that he could repent and cross over into the new. It was a time of revelation and resolution for him.

And this is a time of revelation and resolution for the people of God. God is making the crooked place straight in 5778. He is bringing resolution, recompense, restoration, restitution, and resolution. Chet is a time to know God more intimately than before and to rest in His protection as our wall of defense even while there is destruction and there are adversaries advancing against us. God allowed Nehemiah to build a wall of protection for the people as the enemies of the people watched. So will God allow you to build a wall of defense for the people in the presence of the enemy.

Chet has the numeric value 8. Biblically, 8 represents new beginnings and resurrection. It is the time of new covenants. It is the time of new wine to fill the new wineskins prepared in the previous year, 5777 (Zayin), the time of preparation and separation. The 8th day is the time of Jewish circumcision—the time of the cutting away of the foreskin in the natural, and in the spirit, a time of cutting away the foreskin of the heart as a sign of covenant. It is a time of purification, of the rolling away or cutting away of sin and destructive habits.

Chet speaks of covenant relationship and friendship. In 2018, God was calling the Body together and calling his people back into community and covenant relationship. The warning issued in the letters, numbers, and picture of 5778 called those with an ear to hear to be careful of covenants in 2018. This information teaches the Believer that as God confirms His covenant, the enemy also desires to enter into covenants and deceive the people of God into entering into false covenants, contracts, and treaties.

Watch the world scene for false covenants in the years to come. It may even be the opening for covenant that allows Israel to be divided for a false peace under a false covenant, where unusual alignments and alliances are made, the likes of which are unprecedented. Chet is a time to know God as the covenant-making, covenant-keeping God. In this time, many will see promises they have held to for a long time come to pass very quickly.

Chet was the time of the Watchman on the wall. If 2017 was the year of the Intercessor, where intercessors were affirmed and repositioned to stand in the gap in prayer, then 2018 became the year of the Watchman and saw the rise of the Seer anointing. The ones who were allowed to see and guard and protect began to rise. Also, those who had the shamar mantle began to awaken and come into places of preparation for greater use in the Kingdom. Those who are like Jonathan's armor bearer began to rise.

Since the early 2000s, the time of Ayin, which is the picture of an eye and speaks of prophetic vision, there has been an increasing emphasis on intercession. This is significant, because the intercessor and watchman must be in place together. Many intercessors who left the Body wounded deeply by nonacceptance and rejection are being sought after and are being realigned in the Body. The yoke bar of rebellion has been broken off of many, and they have come back into their places.

We are now witnessing restoration of all things, and intercessors and watchmen are being restored to the wall. The revelatory gifts will continue to increase in potency and accuracy as God restores and prepares the glorious Church. The people of God will remain peaceful as doves while becoming also shrewd as serpents as discernment in the Body—visual acuity—increases.

Year 5778 was also the year where the dividing wall that the enemy erected through the open door of jealousy, strife, competition, racism, and sexism began to come down in greater measure in the House of God as the Church began to break great holes in it through Spirit-led fellowship and koinonia. As ethnic wars increase in the world, love will continue to increase in the true House of God, as among the Remnant and the middle wall of partition, the dividing walls comes down.

Chet is the beginning of the time to cross over and enter a higher level of living and higher level of authority and power for Kingdom operations and advancement. Wilderness wandering ends, and in one day, suddenly, we cross over into something greater. The things we wondered about and could only dream of, we can now take hold of. It is an appointed time. Even as sin continues to abound and gross darkness covers the earth, we shine brighter. We advance and occupy. Our God is unrivaled, and nothing can stop us. It's a good time to be alive in Christ!

> *For by you I can break through*
> *a troop, by my God I can scale*
> *(leap over effortlessly) a wall.*
> —*Psalm 18:29*

One last example of the revelation in the Hebrew calendar is the year 5779, or 2018–2019 on the Gregorian calendar. The picture from the letter 9 is the picture of the serpent. The Hebrew word for 9 is Tet, which signifies the encircling serpent. But it also signifies the womb—the serpent contracting and the womb contracting. The serpent would squeeze to take away breath, and the womb contracts to push out new life, the dream, the promise. In 5779 or 2019, the adversary, the encircling serpent, would desire and be granted permission to encircle people and plans. The desire of the adversary in encircling would be to constrict and strangle out life. Meanwhile, God's plan for the year would be to encircle His people as the mountains surround Jerusalem, to hedge them in and bless them like never before. His desire would be for abundance in 5779.

Until 5779, much focus was placed upon the spirit of Jezebel, and the people of God were taught to overcome the mindset that spirit brought. But 5779 releases spirits of Leviathan and python and other serpentine powers to work at a greater level, and leaders who have been prepared rise to train the people to overcome the works of the encircling serpent. Father God will protect those who allow themselves to be encircled by His love.

While it is appointed as a time of judgment where the adversary strikes with fear as he exposes the sins and faults of leaders, and fear-inducing talk of wars and unusual weather patterns—stronger tornadoes, earthquakes in unusual places, fires, and floods—those who are encircled by the Father will have a peace they cannot understand. The encircling serpent's plan would be to work through the judgment that Father God's justice demands to cause men to curse God, but those who truly know their God will be strong and do exploits. The plan of God would be that men will see and begin to turn to God again, resulting in outbreaks of true, authentic, and unprecedented healing. His glory would be seen again in unprecedented ways, and many would be brought out of fear and into love, out of darkness and into light. The Kingdom would advance. Out of judgment, breakthrough would come.

Throughout Scripture, we're reminded that there are appointed times and seasons, and defining moments. The year 5579 is an appointed time to open up breakthrough for the people of God for times to come. A breakthrough can be defined as an act of overcoming or penetrating an obstacle or restriction—a major achievement that permits further progress.

Breaking Through

The following are things I sense all sons and daughters of God need to understand in order to break through into their new and see the fulfillment of the promise of God in their life. I hope this information will encourage you to never give up on your promise no matter how fierce the battle and to never come into agreement with the *no* or the delay of the enemy of your destiny.

God reminds us that He enables us to do difficult or seemingly impossible things and to overcome things that would overcome us by His power. In Psalm 18:29, He says through David, "For by you I can break through a troop, by my God I can scale [leap over effortlessly] a wall." What we must remember about the obstacle is that God saw it. He is omniscient, omnipresent, and omnipotent. He saw your struggle before it became a struggle. He saw the stronghold, He saw the weight. He saw the hindrance, the disease, the obstacle, the opposition, the sickness, the emotional struggle. God declared your victory over everything that would seek to overcome you.

God equipped you to walk through to breakthrough. God does His part as God. He issues the command, the decree, and says you have victory. He defeated your enemy, totally disarmed him. Now, you must act on what He says. That's your part. Remember Joshua at Jericho. He had to obey to see the promise. God watches over His word to perform it and will cause it to be, but He gives us a part to play. It has been said that God will not do what He has given man to do, and it follows that man cannot do what God has reserved for Himself. We must demonstrate our faith and act on the word we believe, because faith without works is dead.

God said his people would win Jericho even though it was heavily fortified. The challenge seemed impossible to overcome; the odds were insurmountable. But God gave them instruction on how to win. They had to follow the instructions just as we have to follow the instructions. The people of Israel were told they would dispossess seven nations stronger and greater than themselves, but they had to see themselves as He said they were, do what He said for them to do, and boldly go where they had not gone. He broke their rebellion and took them in; they accepted His will and obeyed. Their action acknowledged, "You are God, and we are not."

Accept that this is the appointed time of breakthrough for you. The enemy will work to get you to feel that nothing will change for you and to focus on everything that is not right. Your greatest challenge will be to discipline your thought life to think on things that are lovely and true and to focus on the goodness of the Lord. God has declared and decreed your release, and it is confirmed by two witnesses (the Word and the Spirit). It is firmly established and settled in both the heavenly and the earthly realm, and it shall not be otherwise.

God has prepared you for what is on the other side of breakthrough, even as the children of Israel were prepared for what was on the other side of the Jordan after the wilderness of testing. He has allowed storm, fire, pressure and opposition to refine, purify, and fortify you. You are prepared to break through the troop. The troop represents any barrier, stronghold, hindrance, weight, fear, doubt, lack, rejection, poverty, perversion, etc. You will burst through your enemy's defenses like a child playing red rover.

The kingdom of darkness can hold you up no longer. Light has come, and we have been roused and awakened (Isaiah 60:1). The enemy can not hold back your blessing, for the decree has been issued for release. You will break through the enemy's troops and go to the other side of your Jordan to receive the promise. Light has come, and the hidden wealth of the secret place will be seen and acquired. God gives us the wealth of the knowledge of who He is, the wisdom of the Kingdom and its great worth, and the knowledge and wisdom of the greatness within us by God before any act to merit it. Those who know their God will do mighty exploits!

You have endured. You have stood. Although you were knocked down seven times, discouraged, pressed, and entertained thoughts of quitting, you got up seven times and continued to press, continued to fight. The walls are coming down. The things that have hindered your greatness are losing strength and must cease. The things that have drained your anointing are being removed. He is removing your dis-ease, causing you to cease striving and taking you into the place of rest in His presence. He is causing you to come to the place of uncommon favor where one word will launch you into the things for which you've been prepared, the things He took hold of you for.

Our part as sons and daughters in experiencing breakthrough is to respond to the instructions our Father God has given us in His word. Our response includes dedicated times of fasting with prayer and a lifestyle of fasting and prayer. The fast that He has chosen is described in Isaiah 58:6–14. It is a fast of repentance. To fast in this way, we must stop looking at what's wrong with everybody and ask Him to show us what's been hindering us from walking in and experiencing His fullness.

After God reveals the hindrance, weight, stronghold, or obstacle, we must repent and completely turn away and to a different direction—the right direction. After true repentance, go on to help others. Jesus breaks the bonds of wickedness off you and helps you scale the wall that has been obstructing your way so that you can help others get free as well as enjoy freedom yourself. It is not just denying food. It is denying self—denying selfish, fleshly, emotional impulses. It is giving.

If we will repent for the things done in darkness in our land, He will heal our land and we will have a breakthrough demonstrated in the abundance of rain, natural and spiritual. No compromise. We must walk in Light. We must be real. We must abide in Him. If you're going to be in it, be in it. Be sold out. Let zeal for His house consume you. Our God is a consuming fire.

I remember being told by a prominent minister and a few local ministers in one season that I needed to water down my messages because people could not receive them. I listened and considered, because I have learned that as a leader, as a teacher, I must always remain teachable. And I have also learned to test all things, to weigh the matter. As I considered, I sensed the Lord's reassurance that the message I brought was the message I was freely given to then give freely. It was for a people who would be ready for it. I would be sent to a people, and a people would be sent to me. My message was not a message of milk but of meat. The milk was important, but equally important was the meat.

All workers in the Kingdom must know and do their part so that the work can be completed on time and in excellence. We cannot become carbon copies or cheap imitations of others but the unique one God has formed us to be. We must never compromise truth nor desert our post or position in the Kingdom.

We must put away idols. God must have preeminence in our lives. We must put away the things that weigh us down, separate ourselves from the things that tether us to a lower level than what we were made for, and make less important the things that draw us away from him—pursuit of credentials, ministry pursuits, love of man's praises, love of money, houses, cars, lust, perversions, fear, doubt, unbelief—and never pick them up again.

Gideon, the leader of the three hundred, had to put away and totally destroy his father's idols before he experienced breakthrough. He had to be told who he was in God. He was fearfully hiding his stuff from an enemy that was defeated. God told him while he was hiding stuff that he was a mighty man of valor. He had to be humbled and experience decrease. He had to learn to trust God. He went through a making process and became a breaker. God broke his oppression (fear) and used him to break the oppression of a people. Gideon was a breaker of chains, as was his predecessor, Deborah.

We must contend for the great and precious promises of God. We must do what He has given us to do, as He does what only He can do. Many believers have become spiritually fat and lazy. We want to use Scripture to justify our laziness and call our laziness rest. Many believers think that all they have to do is ask, and the thing they asked is done. But we find in the story of Daniel, for example, that the moment we make a request in alignment with the will of God, the answer is released; however, there is war over the answer, over the promise, over the breakthrough in the second heaven. Scripture teaches us that our battle is not against flesh and blood but against the wickedness in the heavens.

At the moment Daniel prayed, an angel was sent with the answer, but it was held up until, as a result of his continued push through prayer, help was sent so that the answer was released out of the second heaven. We are taught that the weapons of our warfare are not carnal but are mighty through God for the pulling down of strongholds. God has given us weapons to use to fight and win when things are held up or delayed—to fight for and win our loved ones, to fight for and win the desire of our heart that aligns with His will.

The problem, in many cases, is that many believers do not know their covenant. They do not know what is promised to them. They do not know the great and precious promises of the Word. Father God desires that we have knowledge so that we can win. He encourages us to study the Word so that we can be approved workmen who will not be put to shame.

The children of the world are at times more shrewd than the children of the Kingdom. The children of darkness take what has been given for us to succeed and twist and pervert it for their own selfish ends. Those involved in the occult understand that there is power in the tongue and use it to curse, but many believers use their tongue and the power in it carelessly. Those involved in voodoo understand the power of petitions, but many in the Kingdom have never made a petition. If they make declarations and decrees, they are usually just religious exercises in futility with the understanding of the nature of the decree or belief in its effectiveness.

Those who practice palmistry understand what is contained in the right hand and the left hand, but many Believers stretch forth their hands without any understanding of what they're doing. God has given us weapons of victory, and His Word teaches us how to use them. Ask the Holy Spirit to help you to understand His word, to illuminate the Word for you, and to teach you how to apply it. Then read, study, meditate on it, and use it to contend and stand for the great and precious promises of the Word of God. You really are what Father says you are, and you can have what He says you can have.

The Breaker

Deborah carried a breaker anointing. She was given an anointing to lead the leaders and the people into victory. God called her and equipped her. He kept her and sustained her. He gave her favor among the people, and He gave her victory.

She was a woman who led in a time when women were not held in high regard. She was a mother and a wife serving her husband and children while at the same time a prophet and judge, serving her God and her people. She was a servant. Those who will lead well must remember that they are servants. They must remember why they serve.

Through non-attainment and nonacceptance, through financial struggles, and in great victories and times of success and security, I learned to take my focus off myself and to take my thoughts off the opinions of others. I learned to trust Father God and to do everything I do for Him and through Him. I learned that what I do, I was formed and fashioned to do, and no one can do it quite like me. This knowledge came on a journey marked with suffering, but as the ones before me would say, "I wouldn't give nothing for my journey." Father God was with me every step of the way. And He has made and is making me to be what I asked Him as a child: a breaker of chains.

God calls you a breaker, and you will break through. Let this be the year that the breaker anointing begins to flow in greater measure in and through you. Do not get weary in well-doing. Keep pressing. Keep running in the momentum and power of the Spirit, and you shall break through the enemy's defenses. The gates of Hell shall not prevail against you as you advance. Your age, your gender, and your background will not hinder you, only enhance and uniquely qualify you for a specific area of use.

You are a servant, and the One you serve loves you with an unconditional, immeasurably deep, and eternal love. He calls you daughter. You are His warrior princess. He has given you arrows dripping with His grace to be effective in what He has called you to. And you are an arrow in His hand. Grace is flowing from His hand to you as He shoots you in the direction of the mark. And you will hit the mark.

Printed in the United States
By Bookmasters